ART BOOKS

FROM CRESCENT MOON PUBLISHING

Leonardo da Vinci
by James Pearson

Early Netherlandish Painting
by Rosalind Mutter

Piero della Francesca
by Naomi Haskell

Giovanni Bellini
by Julia Davis

Eric Gill: Nuptials of God
by Anthony Hoyland

Minimal Art and Artists In the 1960s and After
by Laura Garrard

Postwar Art
by George Knighton

Vincent van Gogh: Visionary Landscapes
by Stuart Morris

Max Beckmann
by Stuart Morris

Egon Schiele: Sex and Death in Purple Stockings
by D. Simon Eade

Mark Rothko: The Art of Transcendence
by Julia Davis

Jasper Johns
by L.M. Poole

Brice Marden
by Laura Garrard

Frank Stella: American Abstract Artist
by James Pearson

AUGUSTE RODIN

AUGUSTE RODIN

THE MAN – HIS IDEAS – HIS WORKS

CAMILLE MAUCLAIR

AUTHOR OF
*THE GREAT FRENCH PAINTERS AND THE EVOLUTION OF
FRENCH PAINTING FROM 1830"*
"THE FRENCH IMPRESSIONISTS, ETC.

TRANSLATED BY CLEMENTINA BLACK

CRECENT MOON

First published 1905. This edition © 2018.

Printed and bound in the U.S.A.
Set in Book Antiqua 10 on 14pt.
Designed by Radiance Graphics.

Thanks to the authors and publishers quoted.

British Library Cataloguing in Publication data

ISBN-13 9781861716545 (Pbk)
ISBN-13 9781861717023 (Hbk)

CRESCENT MOON PUBLISHING
P.O. Box 1312, Maidstone, Kent, ME14 5XU
Great Britain, www.crmoon.com

CONTENTS

GOTHIC STYLE, CLASSICISM, AND MYTHOLOGICAL
SUBJECTS – RODIN'S "ANTIQUE" PERIOD

NOTE ON THE TEXT

The text is from *Auguste Rodin* by Camille Maclair, translated by Clementina Black, and published by E.P. Dutton, New York, 1905.

Footnotes are in square brackets, thus: [*1].

TO

EUGÈNE CARRIÈRE

AND

ROGER MARX

MY DEAR FRIENDS,

One of you is a great painter, whose art and mind are fraternally akin to Rodin's. The other is the first French Art critic of our day, and has nobly defended Rodin from the outset.

For these reasons I felt it just and natural to dedicate this book to both of you, as a testimony of my affection, given in the presence of the English public, and under the auspices of a name that unites all three of us in the love of beauty.

C. M.

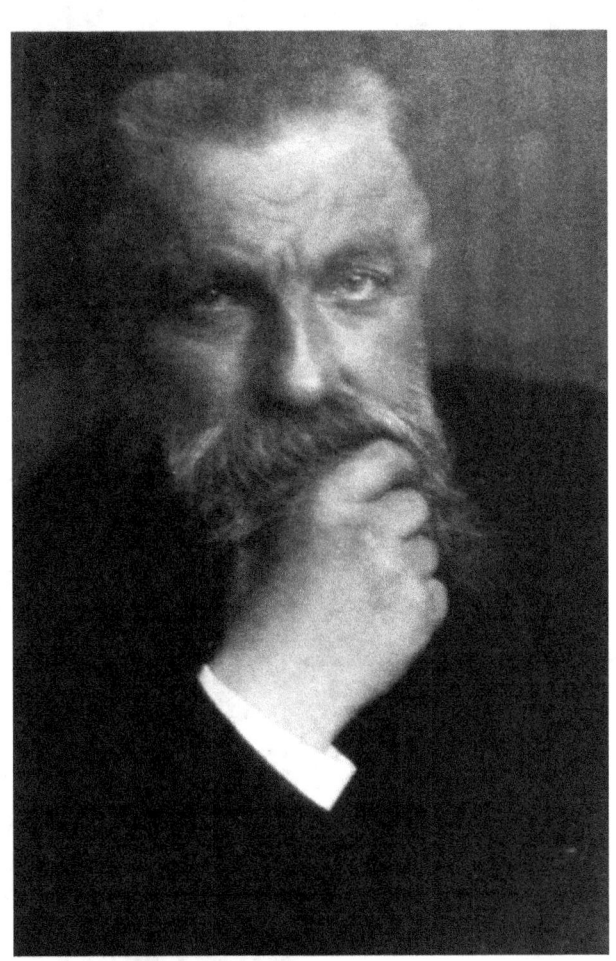

Auguste Rodin by Nadar,
1893 (bottom),
and by Edward Steichen,
1902, Philadelphia (right).

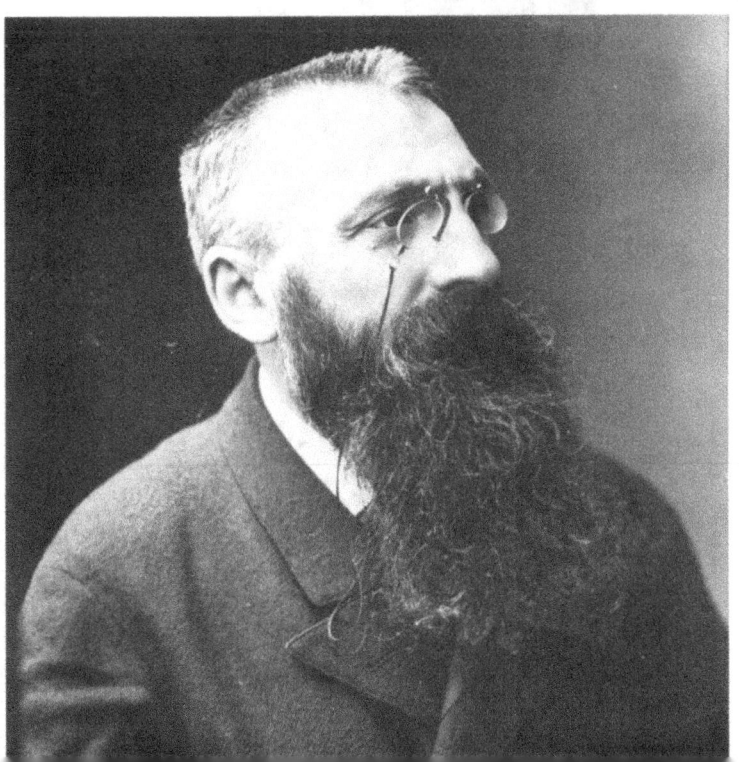

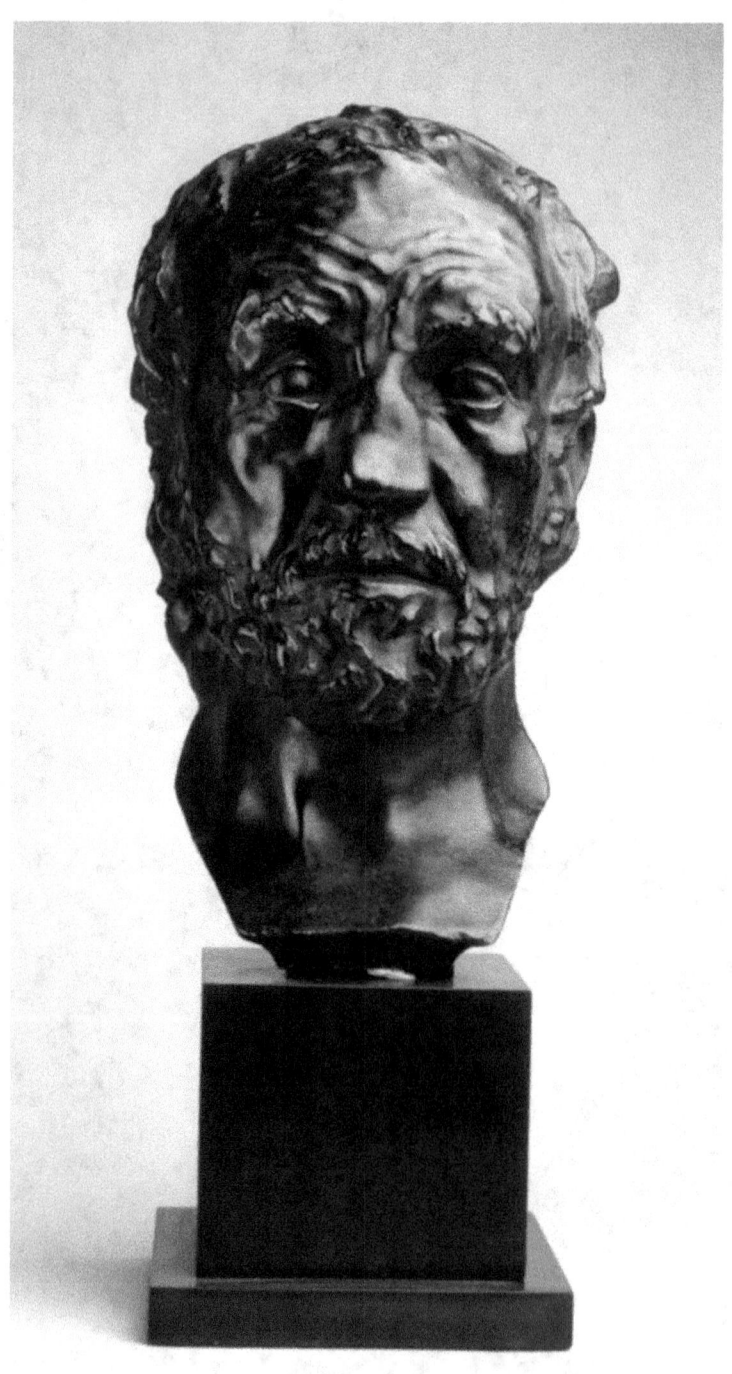

Auguste Rodin, The Man With the Broken Nose

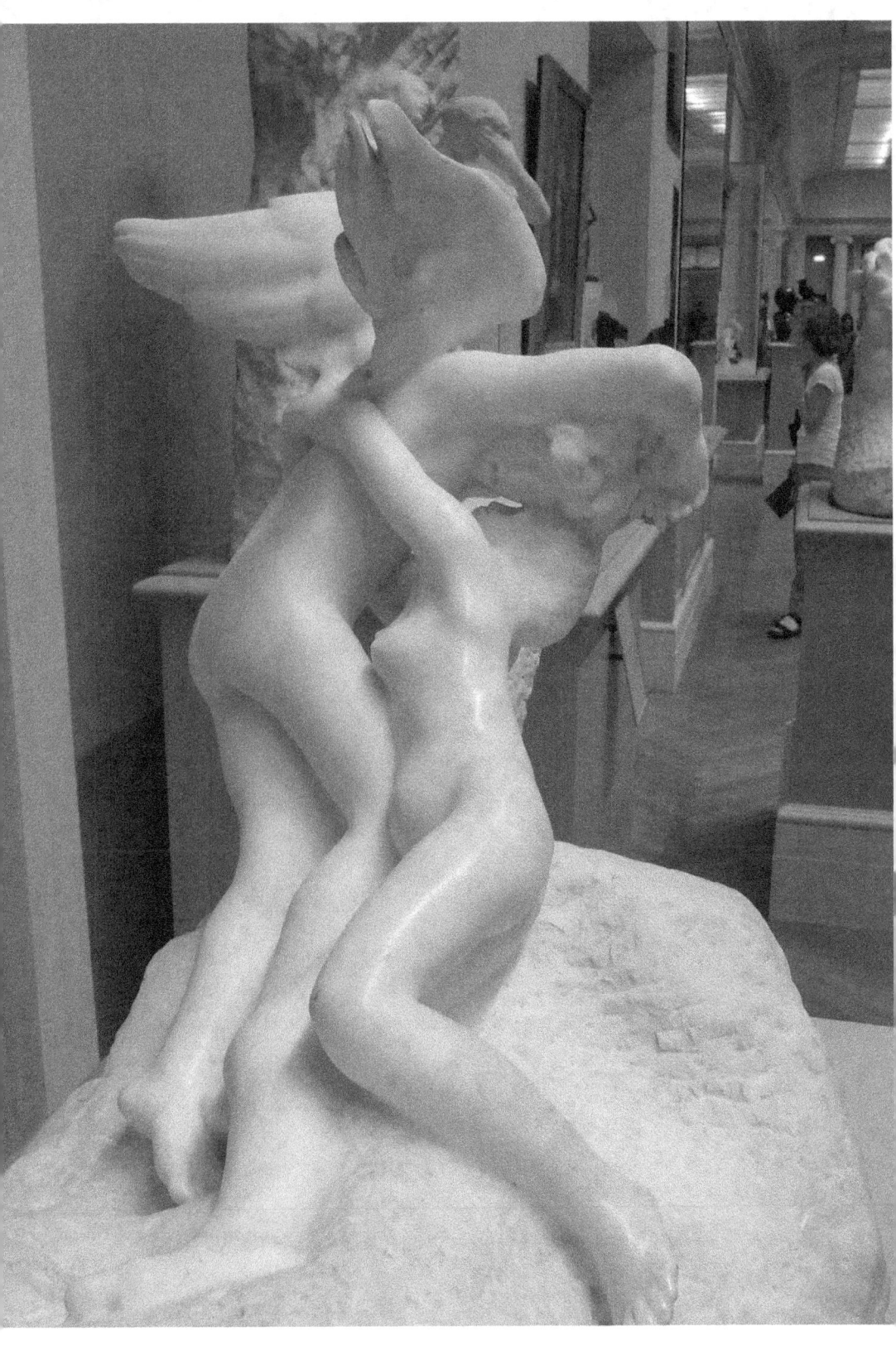

Auguste Rodin, Cupid and Psyche, before 1893,
Metropolitan Museum of Art, New York

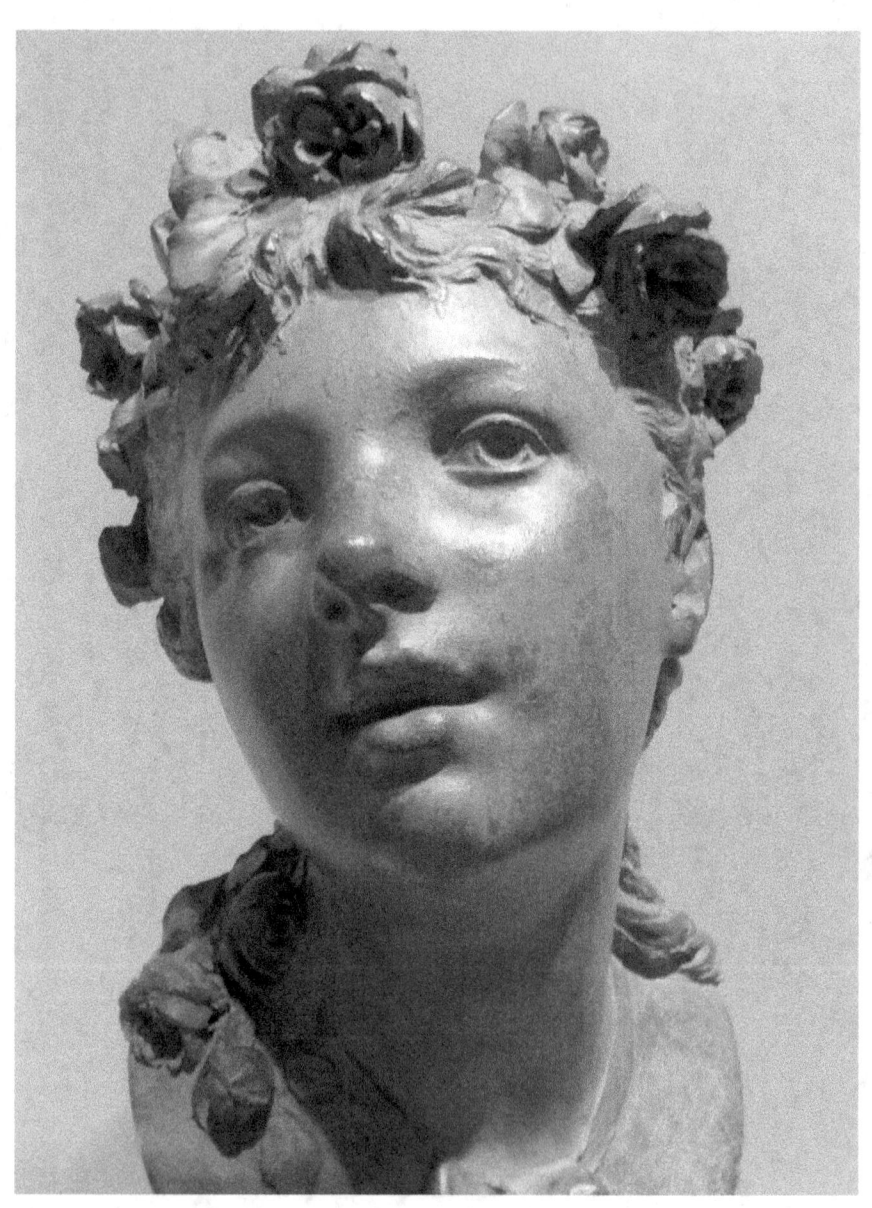

Auguste Rodin, Young Girl With Roses In Her Hair, c. 1868

PREFACE

Auguste Rodin is certainly the contemporary French artist about whom most has been written, especially during the last ten years. In addition to innumerable articles in newspapers and reviews, several books have been devoted to him. In offering the present work to the English public I think it desirable to define exactly the aim which I propose to myself. To begin with, as my limits of size are somewhat narrow, I shall endeavour to condense into a restricted space as many interesting details as I can give, and to neglect nothing that may contribute to a clear and precise presentment of Rodin's personality and work. But such details have already been collected in some French works; and if I were to content myself with presenting a new version of them to the public I should have fulfilled but half of my task and my duty.

The other half interests me far more keenly. It seems to me that after having told the reader all that he ought to know about a man, a critic should then try to make a closer and deeper study of him – come into contact with his ideas and his soul, form an original judgment of him, and in short pass from the iconographie or biographic side to the artistic and psychological side of his work. I have tried, therefore, to begin where my fellow-workers have left off and to say exactly what they do not appear to me to have said.

The things written about Rodin have been mainly literary

compositions, admiring and lyrical passages, to which his favourite subjects have served as texts. Much less has been heard about his personal ideas upon the technical principles of sculpture, or about his methods of work. The reason of this is primarily a fear of fatiguing the public, to whom the technicalities of an art – which involve dry explanations – are less interesting than the results. Moreover, it must be owned that few writers understand these questions. In painting, as in sculpture, persons who do not practise these arts, or who are not sufficiently familiar with the brush and the chisel to understand the secrets of works of art, even if not to produce them, generally prefer to avoid these dangerous aspects and keep to literary eulogy. A work is proclaimed great, and the reader is adjured to believe it so, but it is infinitely more difficult to give him a clear, technical explanation of why that work is great. Towards that quarter, therefore, I have chosen to turn, expecting to find there things to say that cannot be read elsewhere.

Rodin has not merely created beautiful statues. He is an innovator, (or rather a renovator), in his methods of sculpture, and that fact has called down severe criticism on his head. A long-standing friendship, which I reckon as an honour, has allowed me to have numerous conversations with him upon the very basis of his art, upon the manner in which he practises it, and upon his ideas in relation to his own work and to ancient and modern sculpture. To these ideas the synthetic mind of Rodin imparts so much vigour that they are the motives of his work and cannot be separated from it. My desire has been to present them; and instead of giving the public my own opinions, in passages of more or less brilliancy, I wished to give those – so infinitely more interesting – which have been uttered by the artist himself. Often, in the course of this book, I shall be merely the transcriber while he speaks, and I think my readers will be grateful to me for that. Furthermore, in regard to technical points and to the way in which Rodin conceives composition and modelling, I may – and even, in order to inspire a just and necessary confidence, I should

– say that when Rodin exhibited his *Balzac* his first innovation in his present manner, he had so much faith in my friendship and in my critical powers that he entrusted to me the duty of explaining these delicate points in the French reviews,[*1] and in a later lecture given at the Paris Exhibition of 1900, in the pavilion where he was exhibiting the whole of his works. These explanations, in their main lines, I have rewritten here. In that portion I have endeavoured to do original critical work, after having satisfied the biographical demands of the reader. I have avoided discussions of too abstract an æstheticism; I believe that everything can be said simply and in simple forms; I believe also that even in the most subtle questions of art there is an inner light that renders them accessible to all whose minds are sincere, and whose hearts are open to emotion. But I hope that, in reading this book, people will understand very exactly why a statue by Rodin is different from any other statue, and why he made it so – a matter which too few writers have explained. It is not so much my business to display abundantly the admiration which I feel, but which, no more than my friendship, shall induce me to turn my essay into a hymn of praise.

Rodin himself is the first man to be wearied by some praises, and a just observation upon his methods gives him much more pleasure. Like every man of high intelligence, he would rather be understood than praised.

I believe myself to be filling a gap and satisfying a wish by giving at the end of this volume some remarks upon the artists whom Rodin has influenced. He is commonly treated as "a force of nature"; "an isolated phenomenon"; people affect to consider him as a sort of immense unconscious producer. These are absurd hyperboles. Rodin is a man of strong will, logical, and conscious of what he is doing, and strongly linked to the Greeks and to the Gothic school; he has very definite theories, and several sculptors, of whom Rodin's extreme admirers do not speak, preferring to leave their divinity alone in the clouds, draw their inspiration from his views. I shall name some men to whom Rodin is much attached and in whose work he takes pleasure in following the development of his principles, for he knows what he wishes, whence he comes and whither he goes, and has a horror of being thought a visionary – a phenomenon, as people say in their indiscreet zeal; on the contrary, he holds himself to be a real classical artist, whose example cannot possibly be harmful. I have thought it well, also, to conclude by a summary of the principal works or essays dealing with Rodin, at least in France; and by a chronological list of his statues – that is to say, of course, an approximate list, for many fragments of this great mass of work have been destroyed by Rodin himself, especially in the earlier part of his career, before 1877. No such list has ever been made, and it may add to the interest of the present volume; I give it under the artist's authorisation, for I made it in his house and according to his advice.

It is bad to repeat oneself. Yet I am anxious to say once more – and my insistence will be understood – that my long friendship and personal admiration for Auguste Rodin and my gratitude for the affectionate regard that he shows me count for nothing here. A study is asked of me, not a panegyric. When I have reckoned up the vast quantity of work, the maker's life, theories, talks, doings, and influence, very little room will be left for compliments. It will be for the reader to think them. Many people who would have had a difficulty in talking of sculpture have found Rodin a convenient subject for literary declamations – too many for me to wish to imitate them. Such a course would be pleasing neither to the artist nor to the public, and would content them no more than it would content me. Precise details about the man, the work, and the iconography; clear explanations of technicalities and ideas – these form all my ambition. The statement of facts will be enough to arouse love and admiration for Rodin; louder than all praises and with a stronger claim speaks the work of thirty years.

C. M.

"The Art of Rodin," *Revue des Revues*, Paris, 15th June, 1898; and lecture, 31st July, 1900.

I

YOUTH AND EARLY WORK OF RODIN – HIS FIRST
ATTEMPTS; HIS TIME AT CARRIER'S – HIS STAY IN BRUSSELS
AND WORK THERE – "THE AGE OF BRASS" AT THE SALON
OF 1877; THE INCIDENT ARISING IN REGARD TO IT – THE
"ST. JOHN THE BAPTIST"; BEGINNING OF RODIN'S
REPUTATION

Auguste Rodin was born in Paris, in the Val de Grâce quarter, on
the 14th of November, 1840, of a family of humble employés. The
child at first attended a day-school in the Rue Saint Jacques, then
went to a boarding-school at Beauvais, kept by his uncle. At
fourteen he returned to Paris and entered the school of art in the
Rue de l'École de Médecine. A period of desperate industry at
once set in for him.

In addition to the lessons of this little school, where from eight
to twelve young Rodin learned the elements of drawing, and later
on of modelling, copied drawings in crayons and reliefs in the
Louis XVI. style, he went twice a week to Barye's classes at the
Jardin des Plantes; "Barye," he says, "did not teach us much; he
was always worried and tired when he came, and always told us
that it was very good." But Rodin, together with Barye's son and
some other lads, had arranged a sort of studio for themselves in a
cellar of the museum, making seats of tree-trunks, and already
attempting sculpture. At six in the morning he used to go to draw

animals, then he copied the anatomical objects in the Museum. He remembers that, being too poor to buy an anatomy of the horse, he copied it piece by piece. After Barye's class, or the classes of the Rue de l'École de Médecine, he would lunch on a bit of bread and some chocolate and hasten to the Louvre, and in the evenings he would go to draw and study at the Gobelins. Then he worked for a maker of ornaments, since it was necessary to earn a living. From fourteen to seventeen years old Rodin led this fevered existence. "In those three years," he has often repeated to me, "I came to understand the meaning of a drawing from the life, the synthesis of my art, and the rhythm of animals. I remember that a companion of those days,[*1] of whom I have since lost sight, made me see, in a couple of hours, on a very true and simple principle, an observation of the necessary equilibria of movement not taught in the schools, the secret of the plans of a figure. That lesson has influenced my whole life. As for the ornament-maker, in whose workshop I earned a scanty wage, I long deplored being constrained to do so, but I have since thought with affection of it, understanding that there are as many sources of beauty in ornament as in the face."

His work at the ornament-maker's allowed Rodin to earn his living as an art-worker and as a strenuous and silent student; and he vegetated in this manner until he attained his twenty-fourth year, never ceasing, in spite of his poverty and of his daily labour, to work at sculpture. Then he offered himself as an assistant and pupil at the studio of Carrier-Belleuse. Carrier-Belleuse was then at the full height of his reputation as an elegant sculptor, whose real gifts of spontaneous invention were being rendered insipid by his desire to please. Rodin remained six years at Carrier-Belleuse's, and worked there without gaining much instruction. But he meditated and taught himself. From his twenty-fourth year dates the head known as *The Man with the Broken Nose*, which is a masterly work, strongly inspired by the antique, and already foreshadowing all his future. This clay head, which the young man sent to the Salon of 1864, was refused. From time to time Rodin tried to compete for admission to the École des Beaux Arts; he was thrice refused. This disgusted him with the usual career upon which his lack of any income invited him to enter. His ideas, his independent temper, his presentiments, and his love of an art personal to himself, showed him that he would never gain anything, and never have the academic discipline necessary to succeed. He took advantage of an opportunity. Carrier-Belleuse had a commission at Brussels and did not care to execute it; Rodin got permission from his master, who esteemed him, to undertake it in his name, and, after having spent six years in the fashionable sculptor's studio, he went to Brussels, where Rude had already spent a considerable time. He was destined to remain there until 1877, working with the Belgian sculptor, Van Rasbourg, at the pediment of the Bourse, where his sign manual may still be seen, as it may upon some caryatids of a house on the Boulevard d'Anspach and upon some other works.

Of this exile at Brussels we know that the artist retains only kindly memories, but he is too sparing of personal details to enable us to analyse with any certainty this part of the life of a tenacious, concentrated man who, entirely occupied with his dreams, with indefatigable study, the anxieties of poverty, and his lonely pride, had no desire to be known.

"I worked very hard over there," he says, to sum up the matter. It is certain that Rodin was at this time already in possession of that formidable will which led to his success, and also of that disdainful obstinacy which prefers obscurity and lack of success to any compromise. He speaks little or not at all of the drama that was being worked out in him at this time, or of the way in which he refined and cultivated his perceptions, nor of the painting lessons that he took of Lecoq de Boisbaudron, in company of Alphonse Legros, who became his intimate friend; but this influence of Lecoq de Boisbaudron must not pass unnoted. It does great honour to that master teacher who has formed so many eminent modern artists. His seven years' stay at Brussels allowed Rodin to live modestly but decently, amid quiet surroundings, to reflect, and to shape himself intellectually; it was a sort of spiritual retreat that did him good, apart from the fact that he gained a thorough knowledge of the Flemish Primitives and of the Gothic masters who were so strongly to influence him. No biography, however, could render comprehensible the way in which, for example, the brain of a low-born and poor child was able, amid poverty and incessant manual labour, to grow into the wide and deep brain of a thinker familiar with the synthesis of art; these things are the secrets of personality.

Rodin was destined to emerge suddenly from obscurity at the age of thirty-seven, that is to say, at a time of life when many men think themselves hopelessly sacrificed, and when he had already produced much and suffered much; for it may be said that the whole of his work from 1855-75 is unknown and lost, and yet what labour it represents! Except *The Man with the Broken Nose*, none of it is ever mentioned; the pediment of the Bourse at Brussels is crumbling away, time is devouring Rodin's work upon it no less than Van Rasbourg's; he will not speak of the many figures that he made to the order of Carrier-Belleuse and interpreted according to his own free inspiration; and he only occasionally alludes to a large figure that was broken in a household removal, and was, in his opinion, one of the best he ever made in his life. In 1876 *The Man with the Broken Nose*, in marble, was admitted to the Salon. This determined Rodin in 1877 to send in his statue, *The Age of Brass*, and this gave rise to an incident, the very injustice of which was to bring him into notice.

The jury,[*2] astonished by this work, admitted it, but accused the artist of having taken a cast from life, so perfect was the modelling. The practice of taking a cast from the life is unhappily frequent, and we know he praised academicians who employ this artistic fraud without any scruple. Rodin protested. He had had a Belgian soldier for his model in Brussels: he had photographs taken of him and sent them to the jury, who did not even open the packet, and persisted in the allegations. Three sculptors, however, Desbois, Fagel, and Lefèvre, who thenceforward became Rodin's friends, protested in his favour, some critics spoke of the affair, and Rodin's work made so much impression that the secretary of the Fine Arts, Turquet, bought *The Age of Brass* (which stood for a long time in the Luxembourg Gardens and is now in the museum).

Rodin waited until 1880 to exhibit *St. John the Baptist*. Meanwhile Turquet had conceived a friendship for him and wished to wipe out the unjust accusation brought against *The Age of Brass*. The inspectors of the Fine Arts department disowned the purchase of that work and declared it cast from life. Rodin, discouraged, remained silent; a chance saved him. As he was continuing to look for work in order to support his young wife and himself, and to defray the expenses of his art, he chanced to be executing a group of children in a composition for the sculptor Boucher. His facility was prodigious; Boucher saw him improvise the group in a few hours and went, thunderstruck, to tell some of his friends. He had the honesty to declare that such a man, having done thus before his own eyes, was capable of making *The Age of Brass*. Chapu, Thomas, Falguière, Delaplanche, Chaplin, Carrier-Belleuse, and Paul Dubois insisted loyally, and Rodin's cause was won. Turquet, delighted, and free to act, bought the *St. John the Baptist* and gave Rodin a commission. Then the artist answered: "I am ready to fulfil it. But to prove surely that I do not take casts from the life I will make little bas-reliefs – an immense work with small figures, and I think of taking the subject from Dante." This was the origin of that celebrated *Gate of Hell*, which is not yet completed, and which, continually handled afresh, has finally become the central motive of all Rodin's dreams, the storehouse of his ideas and researches.

From that time forward (1880) Rodin was what he is to-day; he had emerged, once for all, from obscurity, and went on to display without interruption and without hesitation the succession of works that have rendered him celebrated. He knew his path, his method, his field of thought. From the age of sixteen to that of forty he had, by unknown persistent labour, been ripening his individuality. And his work, from *The Age of Brass* to the *Balzac*, is but a visible development of that hidden period. The period from the *Balzac* to our own day testifies to a new theory that he has framed. But one may say that the Rodin of the years from 1877 to 1897 was entirely contained in the unknown man of the preceding period. It was, indeed, that slow preparation that gave to the revelation of the works that appearance of certainty, of sudden mastery, which so struck people's minds. We are accustomed to see artists make youthful successes with works of brilliant promise, then we follow their course and see them growing greater. Rodin came to light in twenty-four hours. He was thought to be a young beginner; his past struggle was unknown; people were aware of him only when he had done with scruples and had, as he says, "made peace with himself." From this fact came his prestige. From it came also his well-defined attitude in regard to academic art.

We need to recall the graceful, effeminate, and conventional statuary of the generation from 1865 to 1875 in order to comprehend fully what *The Age of Brass* and *St. John the Baptist* brought into the exhibitions when they made their appearance there. Rough truth, a sense of movement, an intense realism, an absolute scorn of the pleasing, a lofty style, a deep feeling of organic life, power due to the eager love of form, of muscular formation and physical activity; all these things inevitably shocked the gentle sculptors who were enamoured of the academic style and of mythology. Moreover, Rodin was unknown; he had no claim, knew nobody, had never asked for anything, and was a son of the people. That Carrier-Belleuse's former workman should take upon himself to make statues all by himself aroused scorn. His technical skill was so great that there could be no possibility of denying it. Therefore, in spite, the accusation of casting from the life was invented. The accusers did not reflect upon the splendid testimonial that would be given to the artist if he should succeed in proving that his skill alone had created this perfection. The amusing thing is that the same people who declared this skill too great to be anything but a reproduction, accused Rodin, twenty years later, over his *Balzac*, of not knowing his craft! Apart from this question of fact, and these professional jealousies, the style of these works could not fail to displease. In them there was already a sort of symbolic and savage beauty, which has become a characteristic of Rodin's art. The pained, awakening movement of the man in *The Age of Brass*, the gesture of *St. John the Baptist*, and still more his wild face with its open mouth, were so much outside the usual conventions as to make everybody feel that here was an artist resolved to take no account of the "École" and its principles. These two splendid studies of the nude already contained a very special thought. Rodin, therefore, was hated in the first place as a man who would be revolutionary. He was hated because he was powerful, because he emerged suddenly from obscurity, and because he was felt to possess an obstinate individuality. It was also for these very reasons that warm sympathies went out to Rodin from among artists opposed to the spirit of the "École," and from independent writers who divined in him a man capable of expressing in his art thoughts and emotions that had ceased to be found in art.

II

RODIN'S STUDIO – HIS WORKS FROM 1880 TO 1889 –
"EVE"; SOME BUSTS; THE MONUMENT TO VICTOR HUGO –
"THE GATE OF HELL" – "THE DANAID" – THE "THOUGHT" –
THE EXHIBITION OF CLAUDE MONET AND RODIN, IN 1889 –
THE MONUMENT TO CLAUDE LORRAINE AT NANCY (1892)
– "THE BURGHERS OF CALAIS" (1888-1895)

Rodin's previous works, from 1881 to 1889, had been produced in
modest abodes in the Rue des Fourneaux and the Boulevard de
Vaugirard, and later, in a little studio, granted by the
Government, at the Dépôt des Marbres, in the Rue de
l'Université, where a certain number of studios are given to
sculptors. From 1889 onwards the Government granted Rodin two
larger studios there, which he still occupies. At a later date he also
had, at his own expense, a studio in an odd corner of the
Boulevard d'Italie, at a place called the Clos Payen, besides a
house at Sèvres, and eventually one at Meudon, in which he still
lives and of which I shall speak again. Among these were
distributed his studies and his finished works: *The Gate of Hell* was
sketched in at the Rue de l'Université, and there, too, Rodin's
assistants are at work upon his present groups.

From 1879 Rodin worked at Sèvres, having been introduced
by Carrier-Belleuse, and a vase decorated by him may be seen

there. In 1880 he made a fine competitive design for the *Monument to the Defenders of the Nation,* which was not accepted. In 1881 he made a figure of *Adam,* which he destroyed, and an *Eve,* which must be reckoned among his noblest creations – an *Eve* ashamed of her faults, bowed down by terror, vaguely tormented less by remorse for her sin than by the idea of having created beings for future sorrow. This *Eve* is a bronze of formidable appearance and all Rodin breathes in it. As in the *St. John the Baptist,* we feel the effect of a definite conception of sculpture, but here the design is more spiritual and the scheme of modelling simpler and larger. From that time onward we shall find the artist producing regularly, putting forth a peaceful power, and working in complete possession of himself, not free certainly from doubts and searchings, but allowing nothing of the sort to be seen. Rodin's way of working is very peculiar; he does not begin one piece of work, carry it to its conclusion, and then devote himself to another. He has had from the outset a certain number of thoughts that correspond to forms, and although he has only shown his works one after another, he has nevertheless elaborated them side by side, working at them simultaneously and modifying them one by another. Thus *The Gate of Hell* has been made and remade for more than twenty years; thus the monument to Hugo, not yet handed over, goes back, by the sketches for it, to 1886; while the studies for *The Burghers of Calais* date from 1888, though the monument was only completed in 1895; thus, too, among the little groups on which Rodin is still at work, are many that have grown out of rough sketches made fifteen years ago. Rodin has a store of ideas and emotions dear to him, upon which he has patiently meditated, which he has promised himself to execute, and which he brings to ripeness in silence, remaining throughout long years without appearing to concern himself with them. "Strength and patience" might be his characteristic motto. Like all great artists, he thought out the essential lines of his work at once, lines that I shall define at the end of this book. His is a synthetic and generalising mind, which can only begin its active course after slow meditation, and conceives no isolated thing; spontaneous and at the same time prudent. He had that time of meditation at Brussels, not hastening to produce, not permitting himself to express an idea until he had prepared in detail the technical expression, the necessities of the craftsman.

The *Ugolino*, a cast, of which Rodin exhibited the first sketch in 1882, is the first sign of that preoccupation with Dante, which was to be shown in all his later work. He has read comparatively few things, and that designedly; he attaches himself strongly to a few great and profound works, and meditates upon them indefatigably. His whole symbolic imagination has been fed by Dante and his whole sensuous imagination by Baudelaire. These two gloomy poets have impressed him, and it may be said that he has absorbed them. Almost all Rodin's great symbolic figures refer to the *Inferno*, and all his little groups of lovers have the neurotic subtlety, the refined, homesick melancholy of the *Fleurs du Mal*. He has a constant need to evolve from realism to general ideas, from thought to delight or sorrow, and the ideal of Dante or of Baudelaire is strangely mingled in him with love of the antique and worship of mythology. It is, indeed, this quite individual fusion that forms the basis of his personality. The *Ugolino*, which was exhibited, first alone and then with his dying children, over whom he is crouching, haggard and already almost like a wild beast, is a tragic and powerful work. The same year Rodin produced the bust of Alphonse Legros, which has taken so high a place in England in the opinion of the best judges, and in that of the lamented W. E. Henley, whose penetrating criticism paid homage from the first to our sculptor's art.

The Genius of War, the *Monument to General Lynch,* and the very curious *Bellona,* date from 1883; the *President Vicunha*[*1] *and a Bust of a Young Woman,* from 1884. This was rather a period of groping than of production; Rodin was continuing his studies, and becoming more confirmed in his technical methods. We must go on to the year 1885 to reach the revelation of three of his finest sculptures – the three busts of *Dalou, Victor Hugo,* and *Antonin*

Proust, which powerfully declare his personality. These are works that are not disputable, that cannot be accused of having a "literary" intention, mere bits of sculpture giving evidence of mastery and showing surfaces, planes, and high lights worthy of the very finest busts of the French school. As time goes by, the ideas, the philosophy, the symbolism, the "dramatisation" of Rodin's compositions may come to be disputed, or exact comprehension of them may be lost; but works like these will always, by their mere professional worth, bear witness for him. Life, thought, strength, and character are carried as far as is possible. The bust of Hugo was the outcome of some few studies that the artist was able to make from the life. Hugo declared David of Angers to have made so good a bust of him that he considered it unnecessary ever to sit again. Rodin wished to obtain sittings, but failed; the poet admitted him to his table, and merely said to him, "Come when you like, observe me ... and do what you can." At table Rodin took sketches of Hugo in cigarette-paper books; he had a stand and some clay in the ante-room, and from time to time he would run in to note down anything that had just struck him.

In this manner was that admirable bust completed, which (with the two etchings here reproduced) was the only material of which Rodin could make use for the Hugo with the bowed head of his future monument, the commission for which was given him by the Government after the death of the national poet in 1883, and which is on the eve of completion.

The next year (1886) Rodin exhibited the scheme of the monument itself, which has since undergone several variations, but of which the central theme is always as follows: Hugo, naked and half-draped, like a god, is seated on a rock at the edge of the sea. With his outstretched left arm he makes a silencing gesture towards the sea and the Nereids, and thus begs them to let him listen to the Muse of his Inner Voice, who rises, pensively, behind him, and to the Muse of Anger, who, crouched on a rock above his head, seems ready to fly up into the sky. This Muse may also be interpreted as an Ins, the messenger of the voices of the elements, and the Muse of the Inner Voice is also called Meditation. She is of the greatest beauty; hers is one of the figures in which, before the *Balzac,* Rodin indicates his new method of amplifying the relief and systematically altering the proportions, in order – according to an idea which I shall analyse in detail in the next chapter – to secure a decorative effect. Nothing can be more expressive and more supernatural than the harmonious sadness of this great drooping shape; it is really a soul incarnated in a movement of modesty and secret contemplation that disturbs and moves us as we gaze. The Hugo himself is truly Olympian in the majesty of his gesture, the vastness of his heroic nudity, and the magic of the shadow that bathes his face bowed partly down over his breast; and the monument as a whole is of magnificent decorative unity. There are to be two monuments to Victor Hugo, one for the Pantheon, the other for the Luxembourg Gardens, and they are to have slight variations, not in the attitude of Hugo himself, but in the significance and style of the adjacent figures. These two monuments, however, have not been accepted without great difficulties caused by the very nature of Rodin's conception; and the fact that they are accepted has not prevented the Place Victor Hugo from being disfigured by a hideous and gigantic monument, the work of Barrias, which fills the place of those that Rodin had not completed. Rodin's slowness, which arises from the scrupulous circumspection of his mind – never satisfied with itself – and from his habit of working simultaneously at several subjects, has always contributed towards driving away official commissions from him; while the jealousy of his fellows and the exceptional character of his work have further helped to bring about strained relations between him and the official circle. Rodin does not care about pleasing or about being understood by everybody, and he has no idea of concessions. Thus almost all his important works have given rise to incidents likely to disturb his peace and hinder his work.

Together with the sketch of the Hugo monument, a bust of

Henry Becque, and a curious etching made from it, Rodin exhibited in 1886 the first drawings belonging to *The Gate of Hell*, or at least to the work which people have agreed to call by that title. I have already related the origin of that Government commission. In the beginning Rodin had been asked to make a door in high-relief, intended for the Musée des Arts Décoratifs. But the sculptor's imagination, beset by ideas of Dante, soon deviated from the original scheme. The door really exists in the studio of the Rue de l'Université, under the aspect of a vast rough model in plaster and beams, in the very simple shape of a two-leaved door 19 feet high, with a frieze, a tympanum, and two lateral capitals. It was, at first, to have been surmounted by the two figures of Adam and Eve, but Rodin gave them up. He now seems determined to place the *Shades*, here reproduced, in the highest plane.[*2] On the uppermost beam *The Thinker* is to be seated. In the panels of the door and upon the wide uprights are enshrined figures – to the number of over a hundred – detached in high-relief, exactly as upon the gates of the Baptistery in Florence, which Rodin has, quite simply, taken as his model. These figures were, at first, direct interpretations from Dante, in particular Paolo and Francesca da Rimini and divers inhabitants of the Inferno. Then Rodin intermingled figures due solely to his inspirations from Baudelaire and to his own sharp perception of tragic perversity. He enlarged Dante's conception as he modernised it, and has ended by making this door into what he smilingly calls "my Noah's Ark." That means that he is continually putting in little figures which replace others; there, plastered into the niches left by unfinished figures, he places everything that he improvises, everything that seems to him to correspond in character and subject with that vast confusion of human passions. The size of these figures is greatly restricted; the largest scarcely exceed thirty-nine inches in height. The dimensions of the final rendering, however, still remain to be fixed. The splendid figure called *The Thinker* is carried out in bronze larger than life, and Rodin is credited with an intention of bringing up all the other figures to the same dimensions, which would represent an unheard-of outlay and a gate nearly a hundred feet high – a Cyclopean work indeed! *The Thinker*, who has been so called on account of the likeness between his attitude and that of Michelangelo's *Pensieroso*, is much more truly an image, with his stunted body and a primitive man's face, of the cave-dweller, the prognathous savage beholding the crimes and passions of his progeny unroll themselves below him. Immediately beneath him may be seen the most celebrated characters of the Dante cycle, notably the lovers of Rimini entwined and falling into hell.[*3] Then as we descend towards the ground the figures become more independent of the subject, more personally invented by the artist, and at the foot we find "women damned," such as Baudelaire conceived, amid characters from heathen mythology.

It may thus be said that, although, perhaps, the celebrated doorway may never be finished, it is a storehouse of Rodin's creations. It stands by him as a theme for inspirations, and he brings into it a whole category of thoughts and works, never troubling himself about the architecture or the actual scheme. He will be for ever improvising some little figure, shaping the notation of some feeling, idea, or form, and this he plants in his door, studies it against the other figures, then takes it out again, and if need be, breaks it up and uses the fragments for other attempts. Many of these little figures have developed into important separate groups. Rodin is ruled primarily by the need to create and to satisfy an irresistible vocation; he cares little what may be the ultimate transformation of his inventions, and his sculpture is, furthermore, so conceived that it may be executed on a large scale or a small; this is indeed so much the case that it is often impossible to judge from a photograph what are the dimensions.

The Gate of Hell might therefore better be called "the Pandemonium," or some quite other name. If it were to be carried out it could not contain all the figures destined for it by the artist.

There they stand, innumerable, ranged on shelves beside the rough model of the door, representing the entire evolution of Rodin's inspiration, and forming what I call, with his consent, "the diary of his life as a sculptor." To enumerate these figures and groups would take too long; suffice to say that the larger part of Rodin's small marbles and bronzes are but completions of these sketches, and that on account of the essentially decorative character of the outlines and the intense originality of the proportion and balance of the figures, they can be conceived either as statuettes or as lifesized works. Such as it is, *The Gate of Hell* is the plan of a piece of work unique in the sculpture of modern days, a plan slowly elaborated, and of which every detail has been foreseen and analysed for years. No one has dared to undertake so audacious an assemblage of figures upon such a scheme, and the scheme is present to Rodin in its entirety. He by no means forgets the decorative effect nor the harmonious aspects, the concords that the gate should have, and if ever Government should require him to deliver his work he would be able to do so without delay. Twenty years in the studio have matured it in his mind. The work that Dante inspired has assumed a more general significance. Low-relief, high-relief, figures standing free, groups, single figures, all the styles of sculpture are gathered into the symphony of a throng, lost amid whirling mists of hell and converging towards the figure of the Thinker. The conception embraces centuries. Ugolino is there, and so are centaurs, female fauns, satyrs, and creatures dreamed of by Baudelaire, abstract personifications of vices – in particular, there is the extraordinary group of the miser dying of hunger over his treasure beside a prostitute *(Avarice and Lewdness)*. The Thinker, in his austere nudity and pensive strength, is at one and the same time the alarmed Adam, the implacable Dante, and the compassionate Virgil of this frightful unrestrained humanity, but he is, above all, the ancestor, the first man, simple and unconscious, looking down on what he has begotten. The symbolism and philosophy of the artist are independent of any religious doctrine; his spiritual ardour excels in setting free the symbols of the various creeds, and he is supported mainly by deep and incessant consultation of nature, and by his exceptional sense of expression in movements. He attains the decorative harmony of his work not by additions, but by systematic suppressions, as the Gothic artists and those of the Renascence did.

The Gate of Hell is the outcome of studies made by Rodin from the Gothic sculptors, during his stay in Brussels. In this, and in *The Burghers of Calais*, he resumes the deep influence that he there underwent. As to the influence that the antique had upon him, that only showed itself later, in his smaller works in marble, and especially in the *Balzac* and recent productions. The *Gate* corresponds to the period in which Rodin's great aim was to create, through intensity of movement and originality of attitude and outline, a *new system of the dramatic* in his art, which the taste of the day had frozen into a false "neo-Greek nobility," obtained by immobility, by inertia of outline, and by a fear of seeing too living a movement break the general harmony. To seek a fresh harmony in the very study of movement, to create, side by side with *static* art, a *dynamic* art, such, in a brief formula, was Rodin's idea.

He was shortly to exhibit a work which was still more significant of the thoughts with which he was busy. For, though I have spoken at once of that famous *Gate,* which is the *leit-motiv* of Rodin's art, it must be remembered that in 1886 nothing was known of it but drawings. Only by degrees have groups and fragments of it been seen, and the work itself has never left the studio in the Rue de l'Université. It was *The Burghers of Calais* which revealed most clearly to the public Rodin's capabilities in the way of style and of composing a whole work, and I will speak of the *Burghers* in this chapter, although the work was not completed until 1892 and was not set up in Calais until 1895.

In 1887 we may note *Perseus and the Gorgon,* and a marble *Head of the beheaded St. John,* which belongs to the Marchioness of Carcano. In 1888 was exhibited the exquisite *Danaid,* one of the most tender female figures that were ever lovingly moulded by this sculptor of the energetic, and one which has a subtle delicacy of soul that seems strangely placed between two works of power. At the same time a naked figure was also shown at the Exposition des Beaux Arts, in Brussels – a *Man Walking*, which was no other than one of the *Burghers,* and of which the robust execution made an impression. The year 1889 marked an increase of the artist's activity. He was busy upon preparatory work for the monument of Claude Lorraine, which he had been commissioned to make for Nancy. He was going on with *The Gate of Hell.* He completed a statue of Bastien-Lepage for the cemetery of Damvilliers. He began upon the busts of the art critics, Octave Mirbeau and Roger Marx, finished an admirable little *Dream-Group* in marble, in which a young man is lying back and trying to hold fast a sphinx-woman who takes flight, wild and fateful. An impressionist sketch of *Hecuba*, crouching down and shrieking, and *Thought,* in marble, completed the record of this well-filled year. *Thought,* a proud, sweet head rising from a block, is one of Rodin's best known works and the very symbol of his art. It occupies a place in the Museum of the Luxembourg, where it is in company with *The Danaid,* the *St. John, The Kiss,* a masterly female bust, and a bronze statuette. *The Fair Helmet-Maker,* from Villon's poem, is a work on a very small scale, but containing the depth and strength of tragedy – the whole drama of a human body's ruin.

In 1889 Rodin and Claude Monet together held, in the George Petit gallery, an exhibition which has remained famous and which united our two greatest artists. Rodin sent to it the *Women Damned*, the *Beheaded St. John*, some *Fauns* and *Bacchantes, Bastien-Lepage,* in all some thirty works, among which was *The Burghers of Calais,* shown complete for the first time. The sensation produced was immense. Rodin now tasted unmistakable fame, and his reputation spread all over the world. This fame, however, did not disarm the official circle, and not until the last three or four years have the critics been unanimous in their praise of the great French sculptor, whose every important work has given occasion to a battle, because its beauty arose from principles opposed to the whole system taught in the schools.

The five following years were marked by various works which did not, however, interfere with the threefold parallel continuation of the *Victor Hugo, The Burghers of Calais,* and *The Gate of Hell,* which were exhibited in various states in the Salon. Rodin considers it his duty, indeed, to submit to the public the phases of his work, rough attempts, clay, marbles, or bronzes, before the final completion; and understanding very well that his style is, or seems to be difficult, he thus explains himself to the public in the exhibitions, and allows people to follow the stages through which his thought passes. In addition to these works may be noted, for the year 1890, the bust of a young woman, in silver, *Brother and Sister,* bronze, and the *Torso* of St. John the Baptist. In 1891, *The Caryatid,* a marble figure of a young woman with a stone upon her shoulder, the group of *The Young Mother* (first bronze and then marble), and *A Nymph.* In 1892, the busts of *Rochefort* and of *Puvis de Chavannes,* which, with those of *Dalou, Jean Paul Laurens, Hugo,* and *Falguière,* form an incomparable series from Rodin's hand of portraits that surpass all modern French sculpture, and are admirable alike in execution and expression. The *Puvis de Chavannes* is perhaps the finest; it is a work that does not pall even beside Donatello himself. In 1892 the *Burghers* and the *Claude Lorraine* were completed. The *Burghers* waited three years for their setting up, but the monument to Lorraine was inaugurated immediately, thanks to the devoted efforts of that great art-worker in glass, Émile Gallé, and of Roger Marx, who by his writings and his incessant activity has had a most noble effect upon modern French art. These two eminent men, both natives of Nancy, enforced the acceptance of the work. The monument consists of a statue of Lorraine, standing, palette in hand, his head raised eagerly towards the east, and of a pedestal from which Apollo and his rearing horses stand out in splendid high-relief. Thus did Rodin seek to pay homage to the master-painter who adored movement in light, by acclaiming both these in his turn. Fault has been found with the importance of the pedestal in comparison with the statue, the objectors failing to understand that this allegory of Apollo incarnated the very soul of the great artist whose effigy towered over the whole work, and that this whole could not be dissevered. The idea animating this composition was criticised by the authorities. Here, once more, Rodin with his symbolic vision, his tendency to bold simplifications of the general, synthetic idea, was found disturbing. He was asked for the *sculptured portrait* of a man, and he preferred to give prominence to a symbol that expressed the dream and the essential genius of that man, the sun-painter – an idea which was logical, but which ran counter to the received prejudice as to portrait statues. The propagandist persistence of Gallé and Roger Marx, however, convinced the people of Nancy, who are now very proud of their monument. The horses and the Apollo are the most living, palpitating, and lyrical things that Rodin has produced.

In 1893 Rodin made the bust of Madame *Séverine,* the medallion of *César Franck,* and several works in marble; *Galatea, The Death of Adonis, The Education of Achilles,* and *The Wave.* From 1894 date the *Eternal Spring,* one of his tenderest and purest works, besides an *Orpheus and Eurydice,* an *Adonis and Venus,* and finally *Christ and the Magdalen.* For, by degrees, he was returning to religious and mythological subjects, after having expressed only general symbols or pieces of pure realism; and I shall have to call attention at a later point to the original manner in which Rodin was bold enough to interpret these subjects which the academic classicism seemed to have worn out and left insipid for ever.

The year 1895 at last beheld the inauguration, on the 3rd of June, of *The Burghers of Calais* at Calais. To the same year belongs another fine work in marble: *Illusion, the Daughter of Icarus,* besides a vigorous bronze, *The Crouching Man,* a medallion of *Octave Mirbeau,* and – at this early date – some nude studies for the *Balzac,* for the *Balzac* was studied minutely in the nude, a point of which many people know nothing, before appearing draped in the famous dressing-gown which was destined, in 1898, to arouse so much clamour.

The *Burghers* were set up, by subscription, in a square in Calais.[*4]

The monument is one in which Rodin has deliberately departed from all the rules of official art. These require that the effect should be pursued primarily by a compact grouping, the same thought being translated by the same gesture from all the persons. Rodin, on the contrary, desired to leave their full individuality to his six burghers going in their shirts and with halters on their necks to surrender themselves to King Edward, and he has isolated them on their one base. These six men are walking, one behind the other, two by two, half naked and miserable, with their emaciated faces – men besieged, sacrificed. One devotion unites them in the name of their town's salvation, but their characters and their thoughts remain distinct, and in each may be read a different drama of the conscience. They have not the factitious enthusiasm and the declamatory gesture with which an ordinary sculptor would have thought well to furnish them; they are simply citizens who have resolved to fulfil a fatal duty, and are going to perform it without cowardice, but nevertheless were, yesterday, trades-people and family-men with no pretensions to the heroic. They bear with them their regrets, their inner heartbreak, and are not thinking of striking an attitude in the eyes of history. They are the unknown, obscure heroes of a fatality such as often arose in their rough times; and of how many dead men, devoted like them, has history forgotten the deeds and names! There is Eustace de St. Pierre, with his shaven magistrate's face, stiff and controlled, carrying the key of the town; behind him Andrieux d'Andres, with his hands clenched over his sobbing face, turns back, this last time, towards the city. Jean de Fiennes, with his rough beard and weak, old man's shoulders, is listening to Jean d'Aire, who, younger than he, is murmuring words that perhaps confide to him his horror of death, and entreat from the old man encouragement in renunciation. But in front of all the others the two brothers, Jacques and Pierre de Wissant, advance resolutely; and one turns back to hasten his friends, while one exhorts them, pointing with a restrained gesture towards heaven.

The entire reality of these figures is no less striking than their ideality, just as is the case in the beautiful creations of the "Primitives." These are men whose absolutely real nakedness reveals itself beneath the coarse sacks that clothe them, a nakedness not harmonised into any style, but shown in all its veracity by an artist who has chosen models suitable to his characters without any care to arrange them or to give them that pretended *beauty* which would be merely a falsehood and an enfeeblement. These are six wretched men, shivering with cold and anguish. The scene is as close as possible to history, and the faces are real – ugly or ordinary. But an idea transfigures them. The tragedy of their sacrifice gives them a strange greatness, and they become fine because their soul is fine. We guess the gradation of their reflections: none faces his fate just like another, and the reason is that, though what they will is one, what they leave is different for each, and everything in them speaks, from their faces down to the least attitude of their limbs. Their expression is sober; a heavy silence enwraps them; we follow them with our eyes as the dwellers in Calais must have done from the heights of their walls; and they are so grouped that from every point we see them separately, presenting a distinct aspect, and yet the one base unites and uplifts them. This is a marvel of psychological composition.

Technical skill assists this composition; we find the power of the *St. John*, but more simplification. Only the essential lines attract the eye, the details are subsidiary to the whole. Admirable bits of flesh modelling are only noticed after long examination; the substance is scarcely thought of, so much is the mind held at first by the intellectual drama, and this was what Rodin desired. These six beings, side by side, are august in their sorrow, and they move us by means of their simplicity and by the absence of any theatrical gesture. We feel the bodies under the shirts, for Rodin made six complete models in the nude before he threw upon them these rags of stuff and knotted ropes. The feet are strongly attached to the earth; we guess that their limbs are heavy, because, though their will bids them walk, every step leads towards death. The impression is extraordinary and such as perhaps no sculpture ever gave before. This is a reality of all time: the epic of the sacrifice of the humble. As for the style, it recalls the Gothic sculptors by the rugged power of the moulding, the asceticism of the heads, and the strength of the knotty limbs. We are compelled to think of the Flemish "primitives," and especially of those genial Burgundian sculptors and image-makers of genius who produced the immortal figures of Philippe Pot's tomb in the Louvre. There is the same desire for expression in sculpture, which seeks beauty solely in intensity of character, and finds style in the sincere study of reality – all these things concurring towards the greater synthesis of the work's general thought. Rodin there shows himself an essentially French and northern artist, alien from all that the academies, hypnotised by the Italianism of the second Renascence, have chosen to invent as dogmas of beauty. *The Burghers of Calais* is a work of the true French classic tradition – of the national classicality which has nothing in common with that classicality imported from Italy in 1550 by which our indigenous artists have so long been oppressed, thanks to the "École de Rome." Standing before such a creation we recognise this truth sharply – this truth which is the secret of Rodin's genius and of the enthusiasm that he aroused. Better than Rude, better than Barye, better even than Carpeaux, has he found the way to free himself, and to go back, by power of thought and mastery, to our true national lineage.

The *Burghers* ought, according to Rodin's idea, to be placed in front of the old Hotel de Ville of Calais, facing the sea; and he wished the group to be placed on a very high pedestal, so that the figures should stand out against the open sky, or else, on the other hand, almost on the level, so that everyone could walk round them, live with them, almost elbow them. A bad site has been chosen and a pedestal of moderate height and ordinary appearance. The *Burghers* are very fine all the same, and are certainly the most powerful piece of sculpture of the epoch. I have promised to be sober in my praises of Rodin, but I do not see why in speaking of such a work as this I should hide my convictions. Those who have seen it cannot fail to consider it, as I do, the work of a thinker and of an artist of genius.

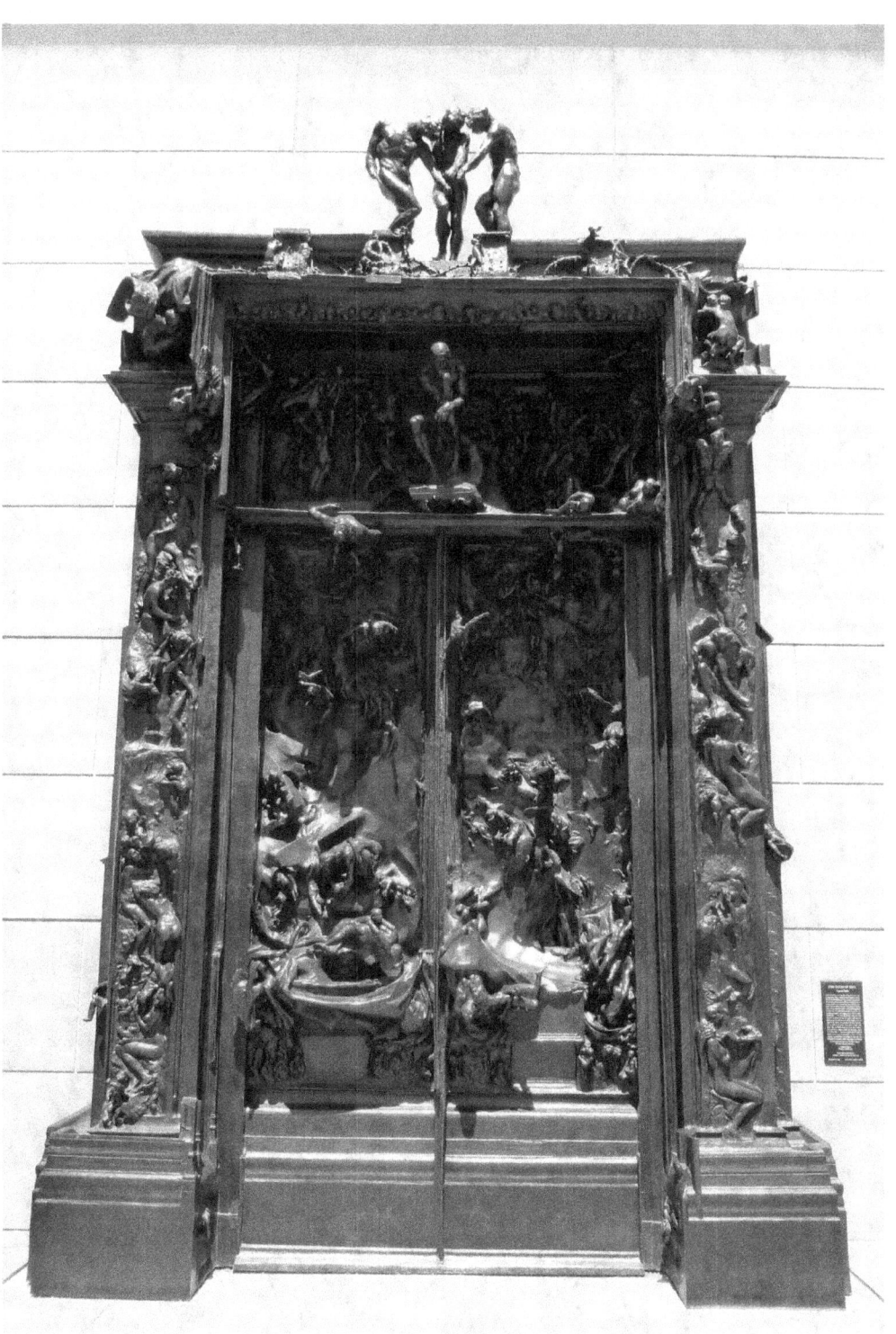

Auguste Rodin, The Gates of Hell (this page and over)

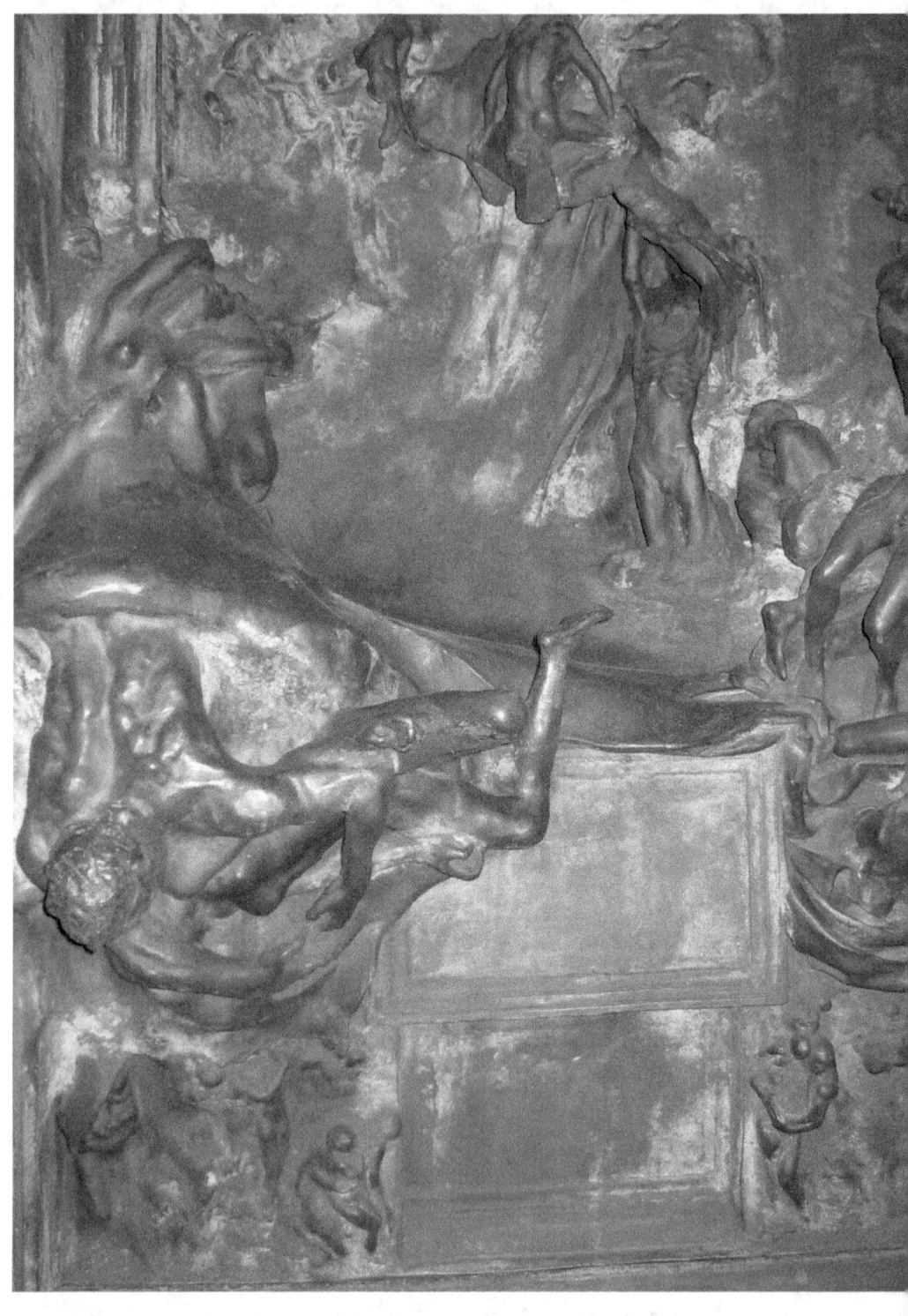

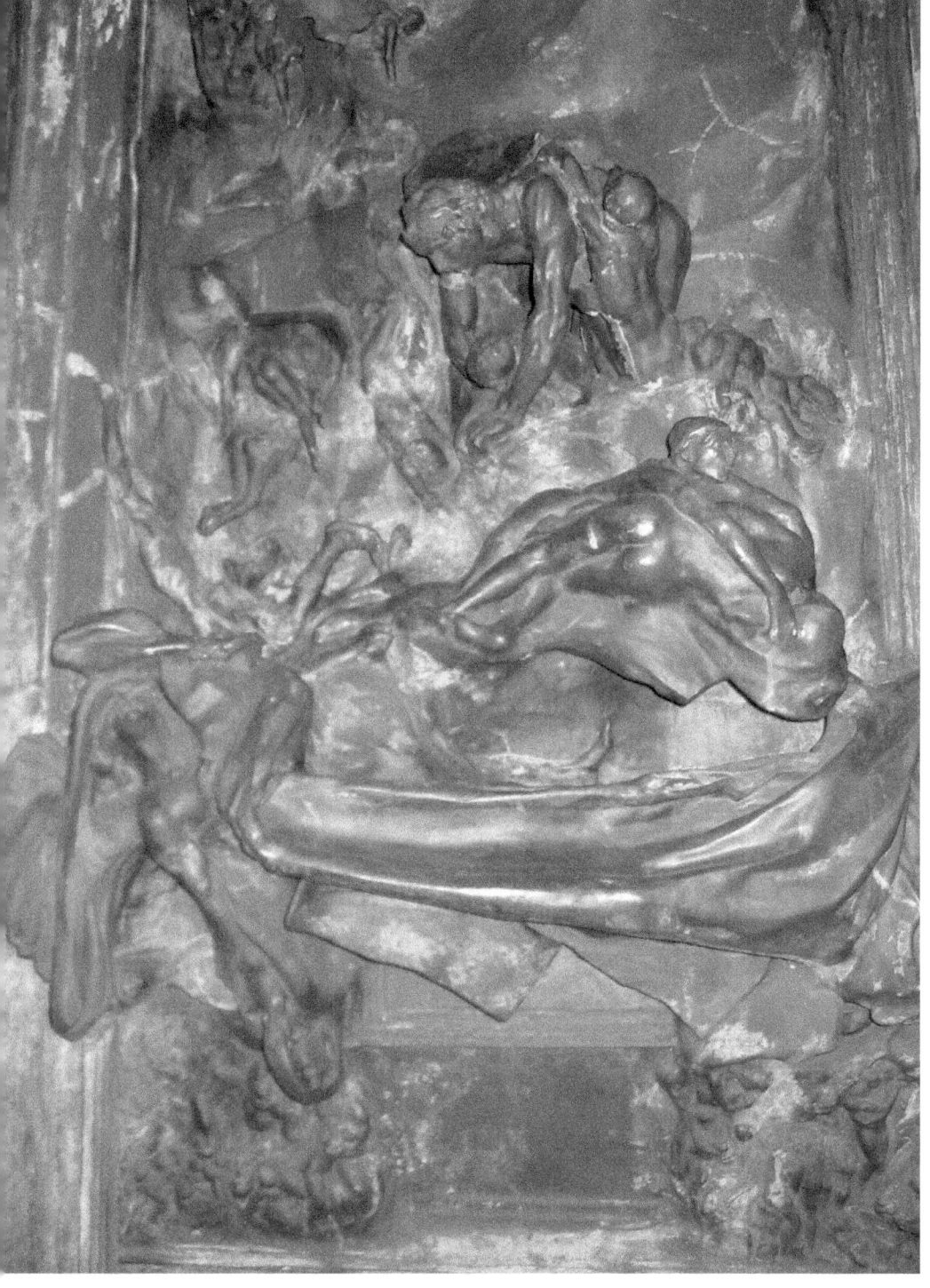

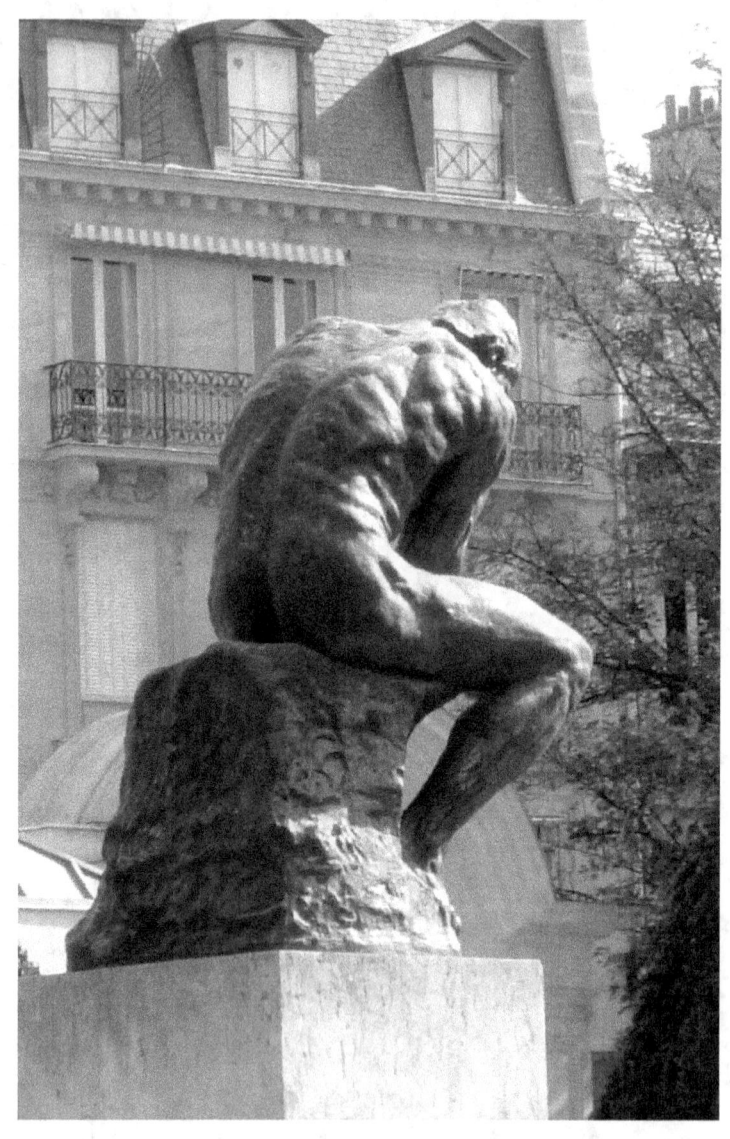

Auguste Rodin, The Thinker, Musée Rodin

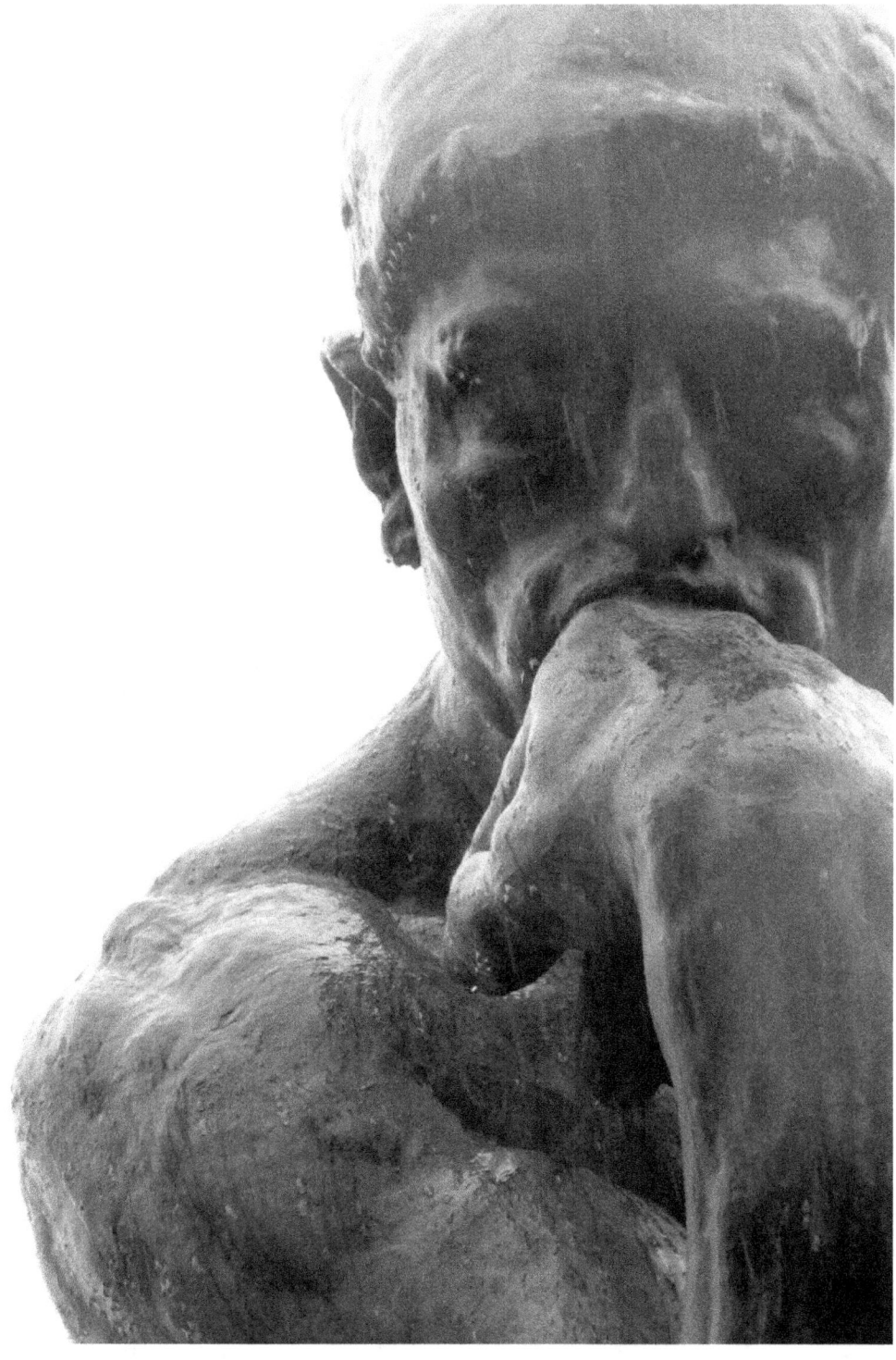

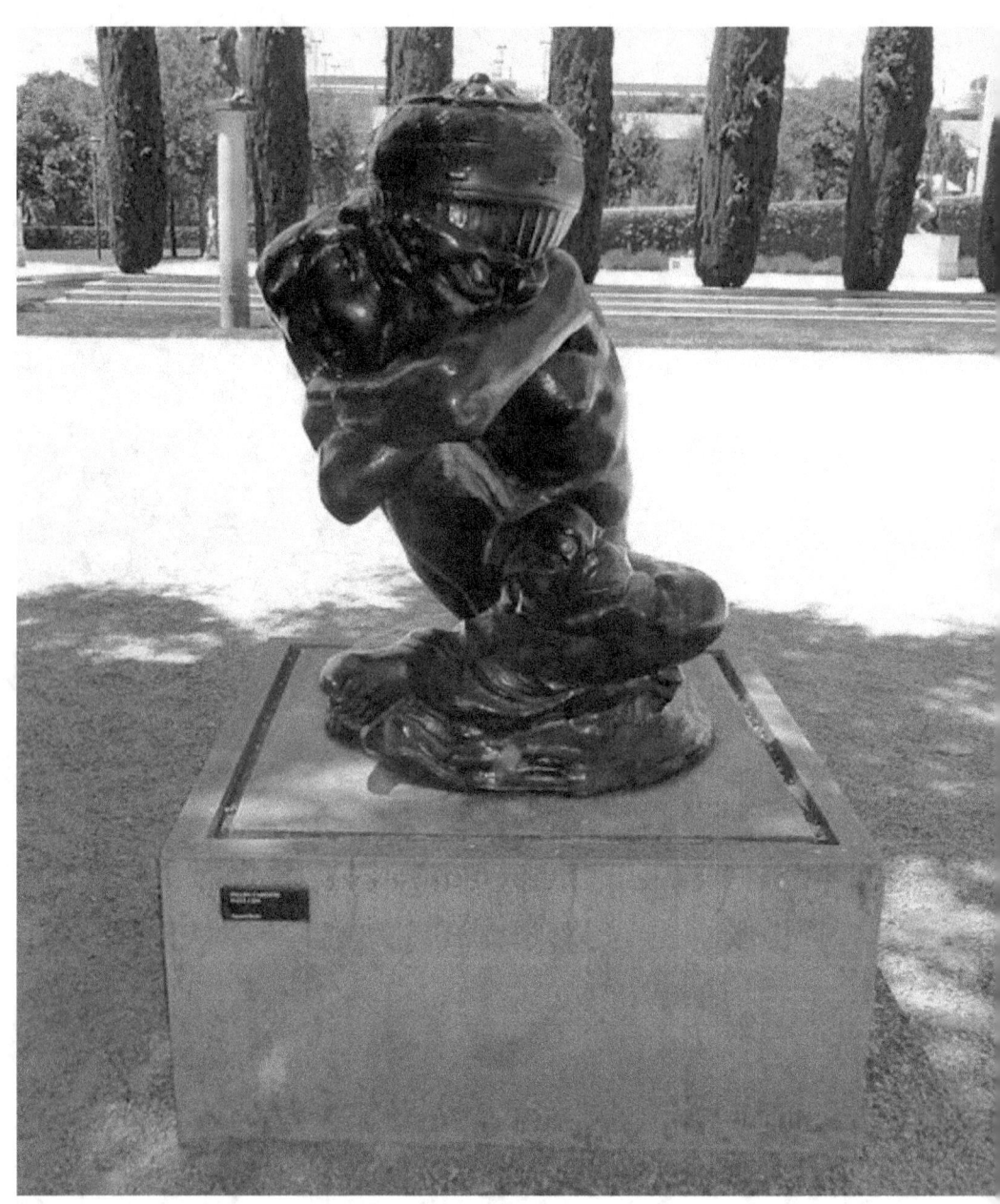

Auguste Rodin, Fallen Caryatid With an Urn
(this page and over)

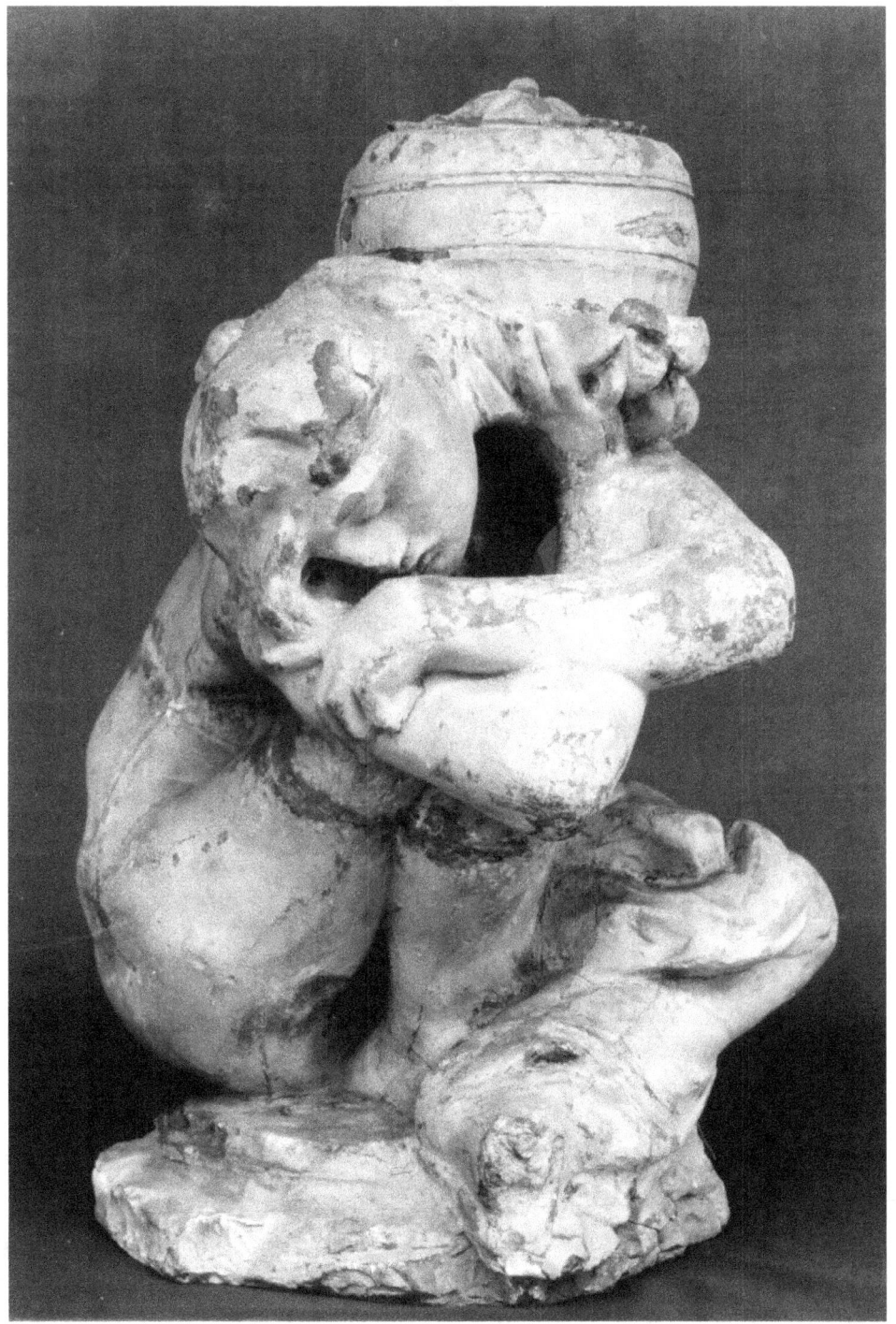

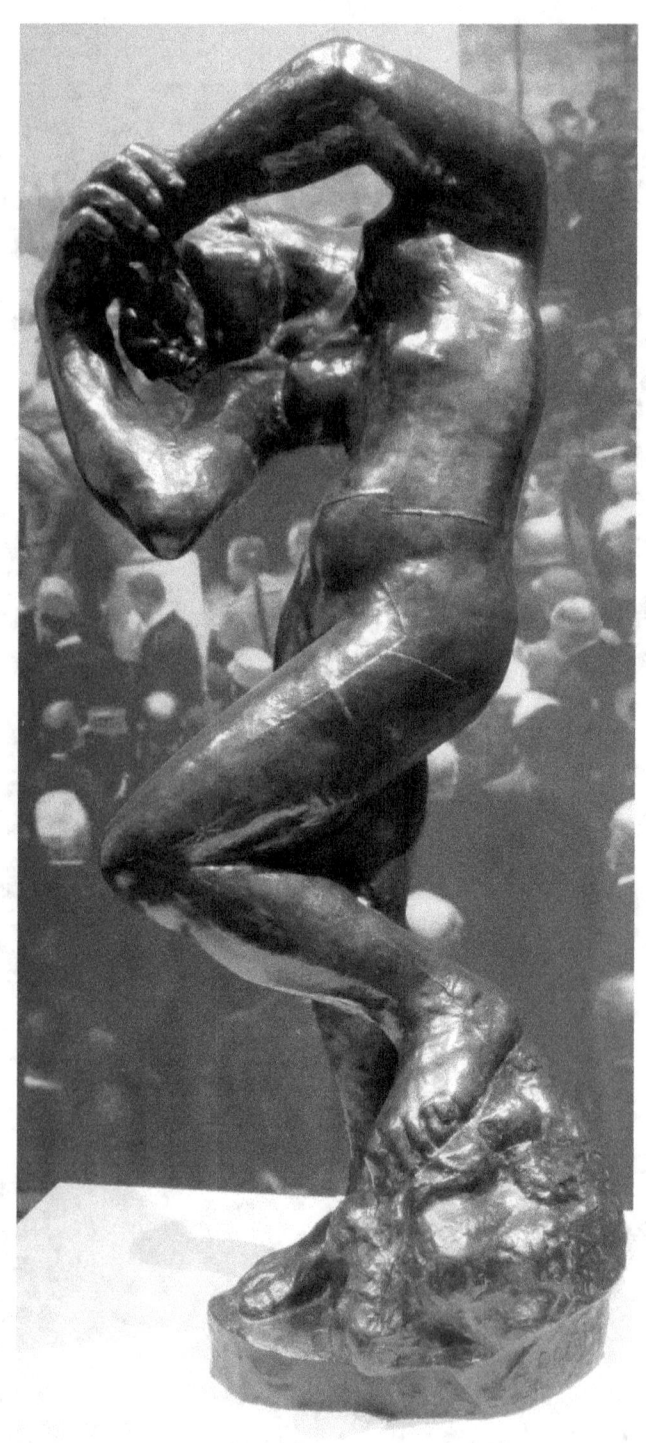

Auguste Rodin, Meditation With Arms, Museé Rodin

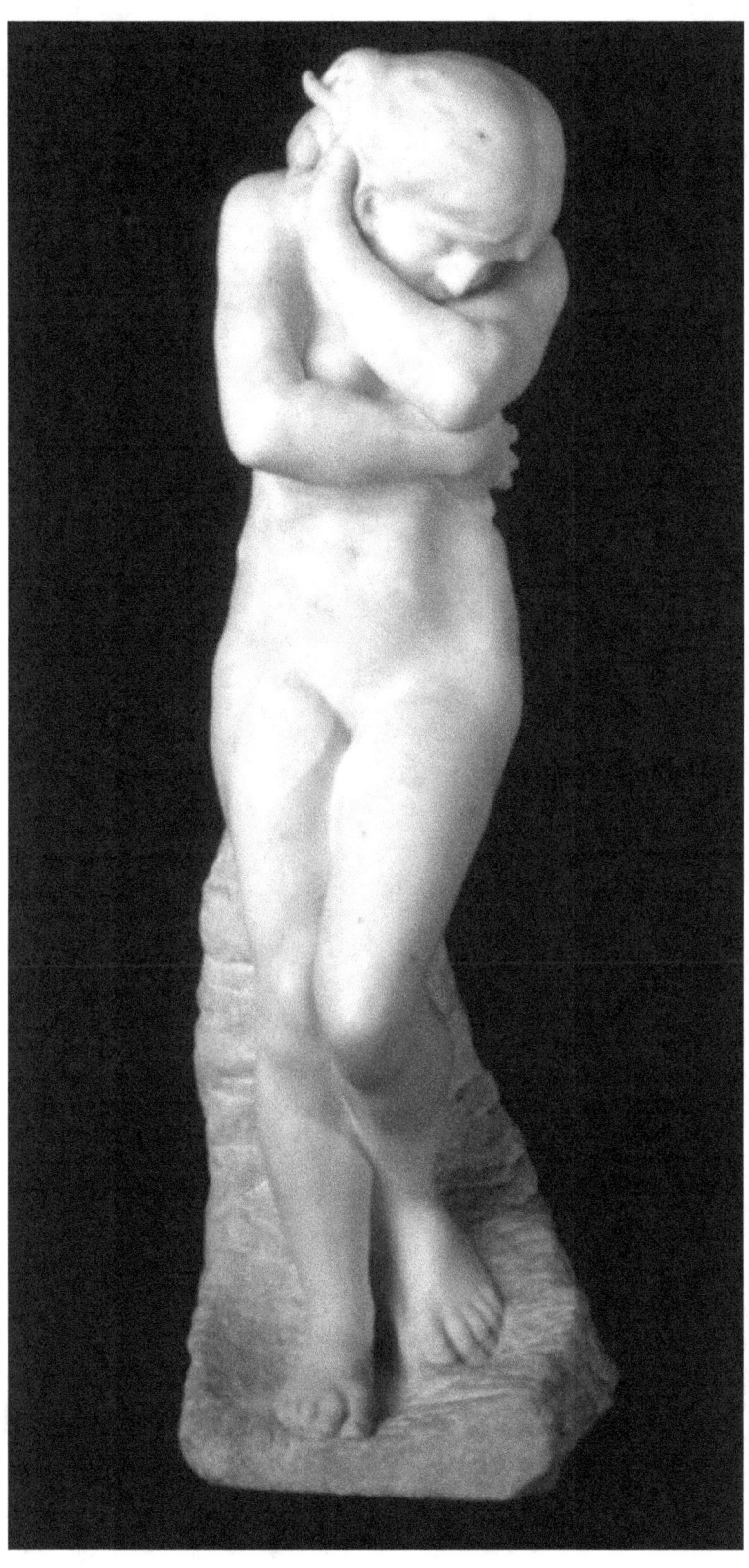

Auguste Rodin,
Eve, 1892,
Mexico

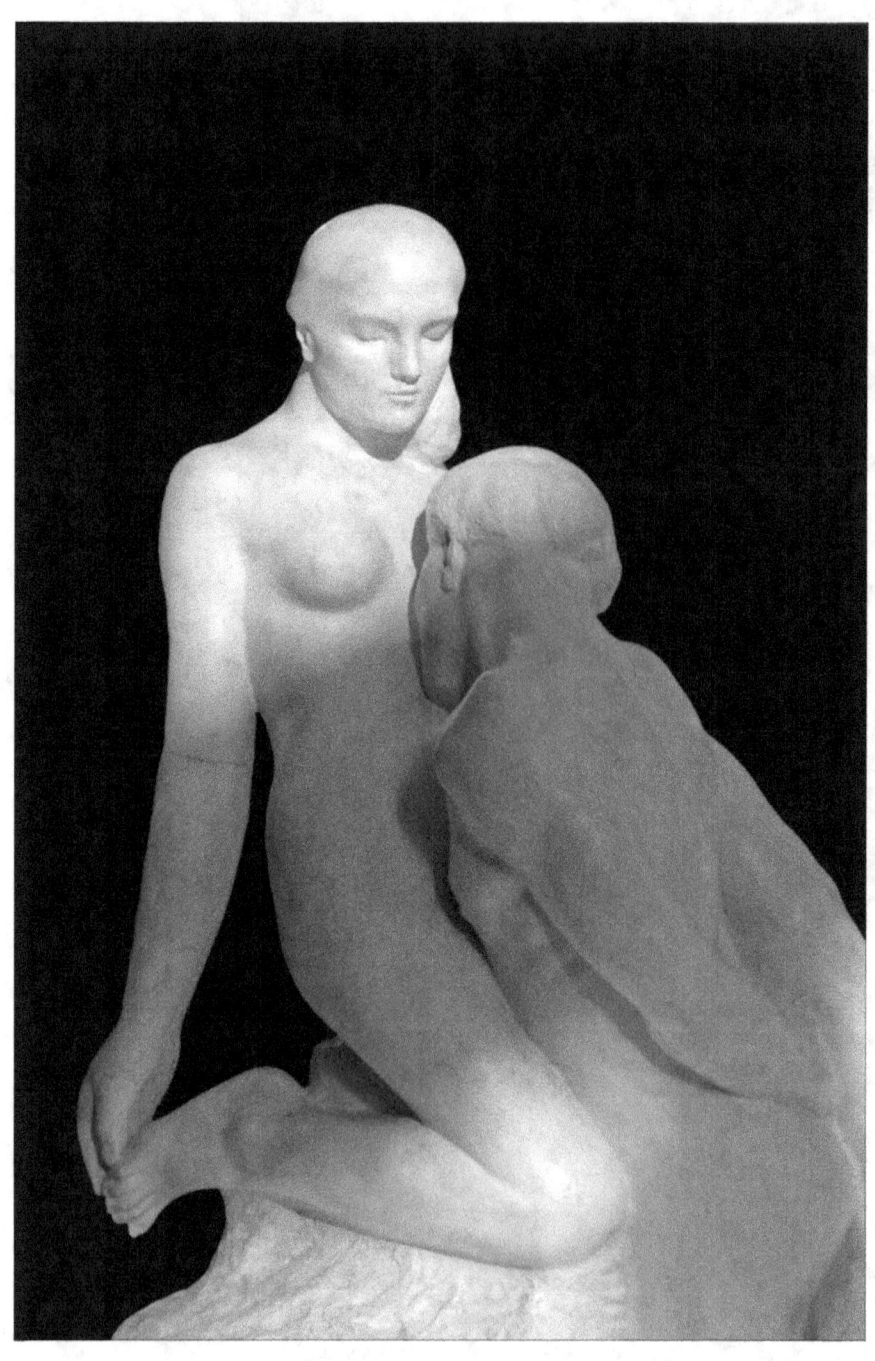

Auguste Rodin, L'Eternelle Idole, Museé Rodin

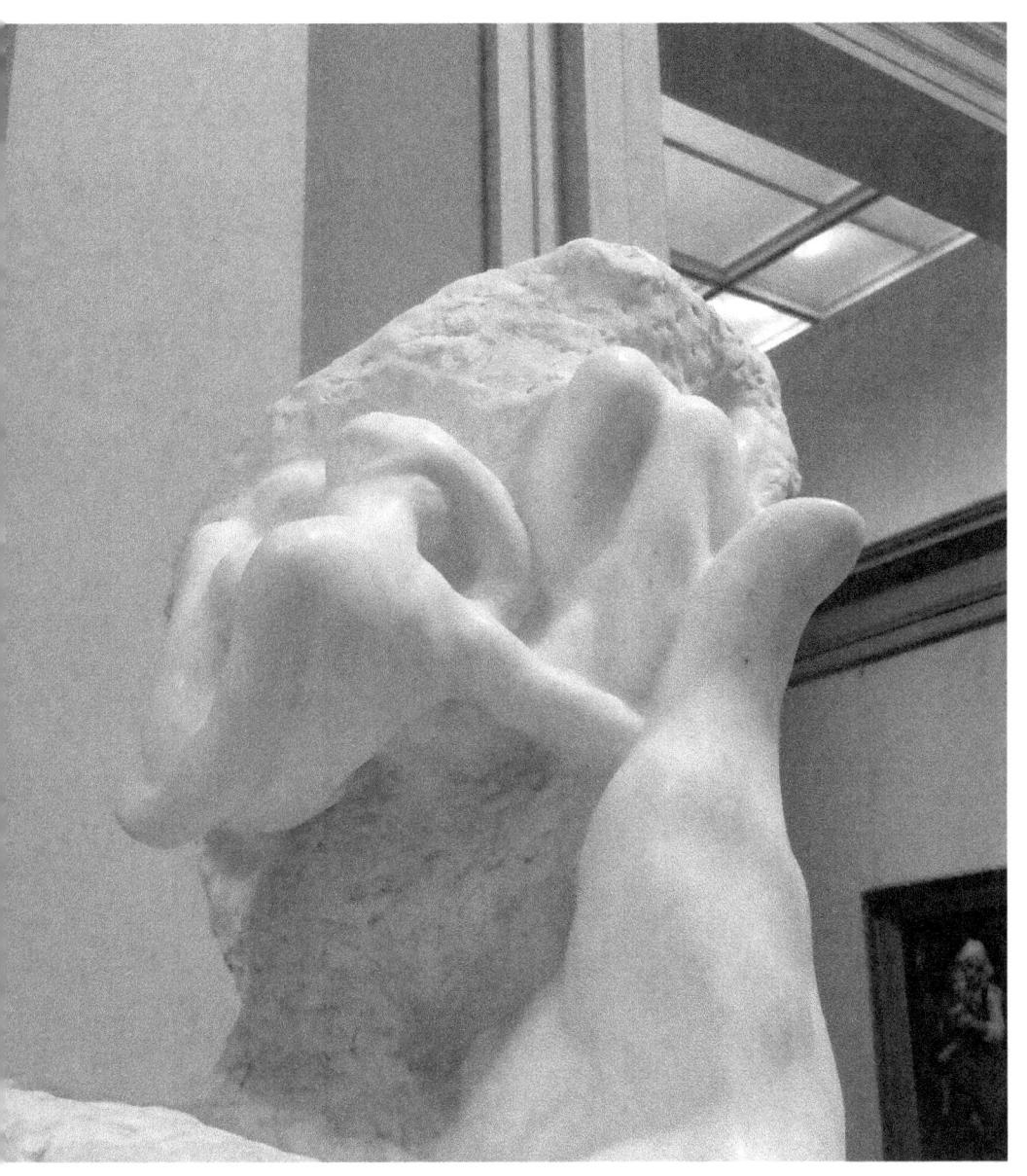

Auguste Rodin, Hand of God, 1907, Metropolitan Museum of Art, New York City

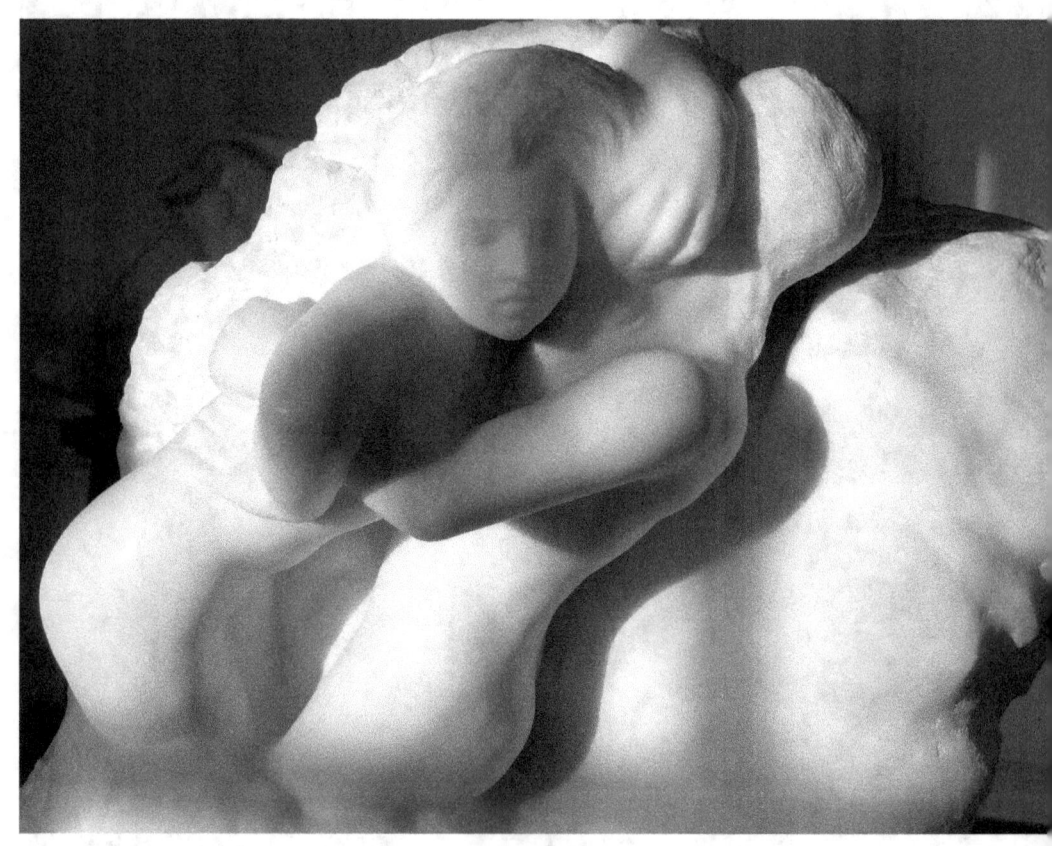

Auguste Rodin

III

RODIN'S WORK FROM 1895 TO 1898 – SMALL GROUPS –
THE STATUE OF "BALZAC" – THE INCIDENT OF THE
SOCIÉTÉ DES GENS DE LETTRES – THE "TECHNIQUE" OF
THE "BALZAC" – RODIN'S IDEAS UPON MODELLING AND
COMPOSITION – HIS OPINIONS ABOUT THE GREEKS, THE
GOTHIC STYLE, CLASSICISM, AND MYTHOLOGICAL
SUBJECTS – RODIN'S "ANTIQUE" PERIOD.

The year 1896 was occupied by the continuation of work for the
Hugo monument. The *Muse of Anger* and the *Muse of the Inna'
Voice* were brought to their full completion. In addition to these
Rodin made a very fine head of *Minerva,* in marble, with a silver
helmet; a statue of a *Conqueror,* holding a statue of *Victory;* and
two groups – *The Poet and the Life of Contemplation* (for M. Fenaille,
the faithful admirer, who was, at a later date, to publish his
sketches) and *The Eternal Idol,* a marvel of inspiration. A young
naked woman is in a half-sitting posture, her head bent, her gaze
lost in a dream. A man kneeling before her, his arms behind him
and his desire restrained, puts his head gently forward and kisses
the idol beneath the left breast over the heart, with mute fervour,
and with a mystic, amorous concentration of his whole being.
Rarely does sculpture allow of so much pulsating life and so much
psychological emotion united to plastic perfection and originality

of arrangement.

From 1897 date the marble group of the *Women Bathing,* the last studies for the *Balzac,* and the studies for the *Monument to President Sarmiento*, a statue upon a pedestal in high-relief. Small groups in marble and in bronze are a form of which Rodin is fond. He has been led to devote himself largely to them on account of *The Gate of Hell,* the dimensions of which necessitated small figures. Moreover, Rodin reserves this form of art for certain categories of works that have a character of passion and intimacy. It should be possible to pass easily round them, to lean over them, almost to touch them and move them about; one should be able to live with them, as one cannot do with large figures meant to be looked at from below. The happy form of the small sculptured block, which the eighteenth century had employed to so much advantage, allows this constant communion of the spectator and the work of art. Rodin, who executes his bigger figures in so large a style, reserves for these a style that is minute but never mannered. The outlines remain large, so much so, indeed, that the work would always bear an enlarged scale; but the modelling is wrought with an almost caressing touch and with a strange love of form. Here the rough sculptor, so Gothic in his austerity, fingers the marble with the care and the delicacy of a lover; he reveals himself as a fervent adorer of smooth, womanly flesh; he plays with the subtlest variations of light upon the inflexion of marble surfaces, and the man who is reproached with caring for nothing but "character" and with despising "beauty" creates arms, necks, knees, and bosoms of exquisite perfection. His favourite type of woman is the long, delicately made woman, with a small bust, largely curved hips, and a face full of will, the nervous, feline, voluptuous woman, of head rather than of heart, such as Baudelaire and Rops have imagined. The characteristic feature of Rodin's small groups is the seeking after new combinations of movement. I have said already that his essential idea was the production of *dynamic* art; that is to say that, finding himself face to face with an academic school that had grown inert owing to its care for pseudo-harmony, he had determined to draw sculpture out of this blind alley and to show, before all things, how the expression of movement might lead to an entirely new conception of decorative outline. From this endeavour arose those little groups of lovers in which the attitudes are so infinitely varied, those curious presentments in which the arms and legs are placed as freely as in a painting. But the painting has the help of shadow, of backgrounds, and of values, which allow the light to be concentrated on a single point and the rest to be blurred. Rodin has attempted so to compose his most audacious movements that, in walking round, a new aspect of them is constantly presented, whereas ordinary sculpture, meant to be seen from a single point, does not allow the spectator to pass behind it. This difficulty and this main idea have led Rodin to treat modelling and composition in a way upon which I shall dwell more fully later on, and to invent a style of statuary which borrows some of the laws of painting.

These thoughts had long been ripening in Rodin when at last he resolved to apply them to his *Balzac*, which was really not his first attempt in this direction, but the first that was seen in public. When this statue appeared in the Salon of 1898, it created such a commotion that for a week the public forgot, over it, the events of that vast serial story, the Dreyfus affair. The clamour was extraordinary; some people raged at what they considered a scandalous practical joke, others warmly defended the new work. The Société des Gens de Lettres, already irritated by Rodin's delays in finishing the statue, declared plainly that it refused the *Balzac*, a decision which led to the resignation of the committee. Rodin might have brought an action and won it, for, strictly speaking, his agreement required the society to accept the work such as he delivered it. He preferred to withdraw his work without claiming its price or discussing the matter. Once again his art encountered violent opposition from the official camp – but to struggle is repugnant to his temper. Inflexible in his will as a producer, he is timid and proud in his attitude towards contradictions. Opportunity, moreover, offered him a roguish and witty revenge. Falguière was commissioned to make a *Balzac*. This put Falguière in a very awkward position; after all the fuss made about Rodin's statue, he must needs produce something finer, or at the very least equally interesting. He was certain of a bad reception at the hands of Rodin's admirers and he was bound to please the others. Falguière only succeeded in producing a mediocre work. The *Balzac* that may be seen at the present time in the Avenue de Friedland is nothing but a half-hearted imitation of Rodin's; it is Rodin's *Balzac* seated, and without character or interest. This work appeared in 1900, at a time when opinion was already beginning to recognise the injustice done to Rodin, and it pleased nobody. Then Rodin, to show that the incident had in no way altered his friendly relations with Falguière,[*1] made an admirable bust of his fellow-worker, which was as fine as the second *Balzac* was poor, and thus gave to Falguière and to the public, also, a silent and ironical lesson.

What, then, was this *Balzac* which was so much detested, and about which the most abusive and extraordinary things were written? Merely the image of the great writer, draped in a dressing-gown, with empty, hanging sleeves; he has risen in the night and is walking up and down, disturbed and sleepless, pursuing an idea that has suddenly presented itself. He is bent forward, his head thrown back, the eyes deep-set, and the mouth contracted in a smile of challenge. The powerful neck – the neck indeed of a bull – emerges from the open wrapper. Rodin made use of various daguerreotypes, and especially of a celebrated portrait of Balzac, that shows him in shirt-sleeves with one brace, and folded arms. The enormous proportions of the head, the amazing strength of the thorax, the monstrous and leonine character of the face are all exact. "His was the countenance of an element," said Lamartine of Balzac, "with a torso that was joined to the head by an enormous neck, short legs, and short arms." These words absolutely justify the statue. Rodin had made studies for it in the nude (there are some fine clay models of the subject in his studio), then he clothed it with a gown (or to be more exact, with a bath-wrap, for that is what Balzac's famous monk's robe was), and proceeded to simplify the folds until he had left only the two or three essential ones. The result thus obtained, with the disproportion of body and legs, led Rodin to hide the short, ugly, useless arms under the drapery, and the figure thus assumed pretty much the appearance of a mummy, of a sort of monolith, from which nothing stood out but the one point of interest, the savage and magnificent animality of the head, with its darkened gaze and the bitterly curved mouth, of which Rodin had made a separate small study in bronze. A great heave of the shoulders throws the body slightly backward, causing it to rest upon one leg, which is apparently bent, while the other is moved forward to walk.

The whole work gives the impression of a *menhir*, a pagan dedicatory stone. Interest is concentrated solely upon the head. Rodin considered that the representation of a celebrated figure offered no corporeal interest. It is evident that a great error prevails on this subject. The ancients have transmitted to us naked or draped statues. It must be remembered that this homage was almost always paid to warriors, athletes, or courtesans; to represent these at full length was to express their fame. Their beautiful shape received fit homage. The gods were conceived as incarnations of moral beauty in physical beauty. But as time and morality have gradually brought us to honour men who are great in thought, the bodily representation of them has strayed into an extremely false path. Dress and physical exterior ceased to be of plastic interest, but the manner of our homage remained the same. Busts with pedestals commemorating in writing the deeds or the works would have been the right form of celebration. But this, the only intelligent form, appeared to our modern statue-maniac ages too scanty. This heretical opinion has given birth to the gentlemen in frock-coats who disfigure our present towns and are hoisted upon pedestals in our public squares. To this absurd point have we come: in order to honour the soul we reproduce its husk, the body, which is destined to the nothingness of the grave, and we represent the shoes and coats as exactly as the head. We attempt in our pious regard for the essence of a thinker to represent that part of him which was transitory. The result is photography in bronze, a wretched artistic contradiction. Nevertheless, if we are to bow to custom and represent a man at full length of whom the head is the only important fact, we must indeed give him a body that is like reality; but the artist should try to concentrate interest as much as possible on the face. So illogical is this style in itself that the bodies and clothes are copied from chance models; the head of the person to be glorified is stuck on to them, and it is the merest bit of luck if it has been possible to shape this head itself from actual evidence! For plenty of statues represent individuals who never looked like them, and of whom no authentic likeness exists, which is the height of absurdity and the very burlesque of an honour.[*2]

In such cases an allegorical monument should be a matter of necessity; yet we behold hundreds of such statues, all the same, and our prejudice in favour of verisimilitude requires us to contemplate the embroidery of their doublets or the trimming of their coats.

Rodin, for his part, to whom such ideas, which degrade his art to the lowest level, are revolting, believes that composition and expression should be so arranged as to make the spectator forget the *plastique* of the body. In his busts he neglects the inevitable linen collar, coat-collar, and necktie. The graceful dress of *Claude Lorraine*, the shirt and rope of *The Burghers of Calais*, had served his purpose well, and in the statues of *General Lynch* and *Bastien-Lepage* he had reduced the modern dress to large bronze reliefs without precise details. Especially in the image of a thinker he seeks to annul the costume. The Olympian character of Hugo allowed of the nude; for the massive deformity of Balzac the dressing-gown was appropriate. The majority of those who mocked did not even know that this careless costume was habitual to the author, and that Rodin chose to surprise him in his home and in the fever of work, instead of showing him in the street with a hat and stick, as they would no doubt have expected.

The *Balzac*, then, presents the aspect of a sheath of stone pushed out by a few twisting folds, which give it the appearance from behind of an upright sarcophagus. The size of the head, the abnormal largeness of the chest and neck, which have aroused mockery, are historic. Apart from these points, one honestly wonders what it is that can have shocked people in this bold and sincere work. The face is admirable in its pride, its strength of will, its haughty irony, and penetrating power of thought. The modelling and the leading lines are masterly. The rather ghostly look of the clay disappears in the bronze, as may be seen from the little head in that material, of which the monument was to be made. It is the freedom, the spontaneity, the life of the statue, which, as in the case of the *Burghers*, gave a shock to the conventions of the official world and disturbed the ideas of the public at large.

It is true, nevertheless, and is generally admitted even by its most active adversaries that this great figure possesses a strange haunting power; when one had seen it in the Salon one could see nothing else after it, and could not succeed in getting away from it. People returned to it, in order to attack it, but they did return to it inevitably. The same official sculptors who in 1877 had accused *The Age of Brass* of being cast from life because the figure was so exact did not shrink from accusing this same Rodin, matured by twenty years of work, of "not knowing the figure" and hiding his Balzac under a robe out of weakness. Besides these reproaches, which were made in bad faith, reproaches arose which exclaimed at Rodin's madness or hypocritically regretted that a man of so much talent should have made so great a mistake. But one thing which the *Balzac* never encountered was indifference; what was the spell which compelled everybody to regard it as an irritating puzzle, as a challenge, as a work out of the ordinary run? Plenty of hostile faces were to be seen, but many of them showed a secret fear of being in the wrong, of misunderstanding a fine thing, a work which was a forerunner. This same fear might have been read as early as 1867 upon the faces of the detractors who stood in a ring around Manet's first works.

The spell lay in the extreme simplification, the reduction of the elements to a powerful unity, according to a scheme with which Rodin had made experiments in silence and which he now revealed. And at this point I am led to a brief explanation of Rodin's ideas upon the technical part of his art.

At the time of the *Balzac's* appearance I gave an account of the way by which Rodin had been led to a new conception of sculpture. This was in an article[*3] that has been reproduced more or less everywhere, and that Rodin has been good enough to consider as the emanation and direct expression of his artistic wishes. I cannot enter into all the details. The scale of this book would not allow of that, but the following are the principal points of that evolution.

Rodin's is above all a temperament inclined to the expression of passionate and tragic character. Thence comes his constant study of movement. As I said before, that study has led him to give unlooked-for values to the general outline and to produce works which may be viewed on all sides and which continually show a fresh and balanced aspect that explains the other aspects: otherwise the daring gestures and the bold combinations of the limbs would have given an air of absurdity to the groups. Rodin is at the same time very reflective and very instinctive. He matures a thought slowly, but he often passes by chance from that thought to its realisation. This is the predominant feature of his nature, and it explains his entire art. Rodin often appears unconscious, astonished at what he had in him and at what he has brought into existence, to such a degree that he explains it badly enough. He sees his thought in the whole of nature and finds it there again; that thought, indeed, is fed by general ideas, and is, if I may say so, almost "elemental." From this point of view Rodin's *genius* is independent of his *talent* as a sculptor. It sometimes happens to him to see a block of marble or a knob of wood, and the form of such an object will show him what he will make and the movement of the figure. He adapts to it one of the ideas which he always has in reserve: the aspect of the wood or the marble determines the passage of the thought to the material which will incarnate it. I said one day to Rodin: "One would say that you knew there was a figure in that block, and that you do nothing beyond breaking away the stone that hides it from us." He answered that that was exactly his feeling as he worked. Upon the naked figure Rodin has ideas that are peculiar to his nature as a mystic and a realist. He considers the body with its four limbs as a cypher, of which the combinations are infinite. That is an old idea that was held by primitive theologians of the Eastern religions. And it is the fact that Rodin has invented an immense series of attitudes and combinations that one would not have thought possible: he attaches little groups to the side of a block of marble with the freedom of a painter throwing a figure upon a background. He makes his people light, he makes them soar, he entwines them in surprising positions.

It was therefore absolutely essential that he should find means to constitute a logical harmony *on every side* of his works. Scholastic statuary is opposed to this principle. Its tendency is to treat groups as bas-reliefs. The spectator must stand in front, at a certain spot, and whatever is behind is accessory: the decorative line produces its effect only from that point. So true is this that statues are very often so placed in public squares that people cannot pass round them. The academic sculptors treat a piece of sculpture like a picture; it has a right side and a wrong side. Rodin, shocked at this method, began by working in quite a different way. He made successive sketches of all the faces of his works, going constantly round them so as to obtain a series of views connected in a ring. Travels in Italy had led him to think that the ancients proceeded in this manner and that their great endeavour was to get the design of the outline by means of movement, which continually modifies the anatomy. Anatomy, indispensable to the artist, becomes the source of all the academic errors if once we forget that it is but inertia, the state of non-action, and consequently incapable of expressly teaching us about life and about the modifications that thought imposes upon flesh. The real value of a living figure is given by profiles studied successively in a full light. Rodin was delighted by this way of working. But his pictorial inclinations, his ideas about the possible formation of a *background* in sculpture as in painting, were not satisfied.

When the academic school wishes to make use of a background to a figure it confines itself to a hollow or a relief. Rodin desired that a statue should stand free and should bear looking at from any point, but he desired nevertheless that it should remain in relation with light and with the surrounding atmosphere. He was struck by the hard, cut-out aspect of ordinary statues, and asked himself how an atmosphere might be given to them. Painting has two means to this end: of which the first is *values*. *Values* are independent of colour. Values, an element common to both arts, are in painting and sculpture *the relations as to opacity or transparence of an object and the background against which it is seen.* They may be dark on a light ground, light on a dark ground, or light upon a ground that is likewise light; but they are always the very life of the outline, and the important point is to fix that outline first of all. When we see a person placed between the sun and ourselves, against the light, we do not at first perceive the details within the outline, but we do see the general mass of the body, and that mass is filled with more or less intense colour, in which we presently distinguish details. Our perception at the moment is as much sculptural as pictorial. Rodin, struck by the importance of this idea, devoted himself to obtaining, *at once and together,* the *volume;* that is to say, the equivalent in sculpture of the *value,* and the design of *successive views of one movement.*

But the second means in painting is the employment of intermediate tones encircling the figure and combining with the background. How could an equivalent be found for that? Logic led Rodin on to a step which alarmed him: he made experiments after examining the antiques very closely. He took fragments of his statues and began to raise them in certain places by layers of clay, intensifying the modelling and enlarging the lines. He observed that the light now played better upon these enlarged lines; the refraction of light upon these amplified surfaces was softer, the hardness of the cut-out outline vanished, and a radiant zone shaped itself around his figures and united them gradually with the atmosphere. In this way, therefore, by means of this systematic accentuation of the outlines, an intermediate tone, *a radiancy of the forms,* was produced.

Rodin understood at once that he had found his way to the deepest secret of his art; that is to say, to the ideal limit where through its hidden laws a plastic art touches the other arts in a negation of all that is merely materialistic. The intermediate tones in painting, the radiating surfaces in sculpture, are the same principle as the nervous radiations noted in photographing a hand, where it may be seen that the fingers are prolonged by emanations. Nothing is fixed, limited, or finished in nature, and the radiating state is the only real one. But this was a dangerous discovery for a sculptor, since people would immediately exclaim upon the *deformation of what was seen,* the alteration of the fact, the falsification of anatomy. Therefore Rodin proceeded in silence and with very great prudence. The point was not, of course, *to enlarge all surfaces equally,* for that would have produced only an increase of scale. The thing was *to amplify,* with tact, *certain parts of the modelling,* the edges of which were swept by the light, so as to give a halo to the outline. At the same time, Rodin experimented in a series of drawings made on purpose, forbidding himself to give any detail, tracing only the outlines of bodies filled in with one wash of water-colour that gave the *value.* I shall return to these sketches. They cannot be understood without a knowledge of their original purpose.

This theory, to which Rodin approved of my giving the name of *deliberate amplification of surfaces,* is simply the critical principle of Greek sculpture, which has been entirely misunderstood by the academic school. That school, which is supposed to honour the Greeks, is really false to their spirit and their teaching. Moreover, this principle, which belongs to all the primitive statuary that was made for the open air, is to be found among the Egyptians and the Assyrians. It calls in question the academic tradition whereby *exactitude* is confounded with *truth*. In reality it may be said to be a profoundly classic principle which has been denied by the academic school. Here, as in painting, classicism is opposed to the academic. Hence it should be concluded that in reality Rodin is by no means an *innovator* opposing himself to a school that retains classic traditions, but, speaking precisely, a classic, returning to nature, replacing himself in the state of mind of a Greek before his model, and opposing himself to a school that has overloaded art with methods, formulas, and expedients that change the character of antique and Gothic art. Rodin has a horror of what is called "originality," and an even greater horror of what is called "inspiration." He only trusts completely to work and to minute, sincere observation of nature. "Slowness is a beauty," he often says. He has the greatest antipathy for "sculpture with literary meanings," and has often been galled, without saying so, by certain praises, in which writers, reeling off pages of description about his works, have thought to please him by dwelling on the idea and not on the execution. "I invent nothing," he says; "I rediscover. And the thing seems new because people have generally lost sight of the aim and the means of art; they take that for an innovation which is nothing but a return to the laws of the great sculpture of long ago. Obviously, I think; I like certain symbols, I see things in a synthetic way, but it is nature that gives me all that. I do not imitate the Greeks; I try to put myself in the spiritual state of the men who have left us the antique statues. The 'École' copies their works; the thing that signifies is to *recover their method*. I began by showing close studies from nature like *The Age of Brass*. Afterwards I came to understand that art required a little more largeness, a little exaggeration, and my whole aim, from the time of the *Burghers*, was to find a method of exaggerating logically: that method consists in the deliberate amplification of the modelling. It consists also in the constant reduction of the figure to a geometrical figure, and in the determination to sacrifice any part of a figure to the synthesis of its aspect. See what the Gothic sculptors did. Look at the cathedral of Chartres; one of the towers is massive and without ornament: they sacrificed it to give value to the exquisite delicacy of the other tower.

"In sculpture the projection of the muscular *fasciculi* must be accentuated, the foreshortening forced, the hollows deepened; sculpture is the art of the hole and the lump, not of clear, well-smoothed, unmodelled figures. Ignorant people, when they see close-knitted true surfaces, say that 'it is not finished.' No notion is falser than that of *finish* unless it be that of *elegance*; by means of these two ideas people would kill our art. The way to obtain solidity and life is by work carried out to the fullest, not in the direction of achievement and of copying details, but in that of truth in the successive schemes. The public, perverted by academic prejudices, confounds art with neatness. The simplicity of the 'École' is a painted cardboard ideal. A cast from life is a copy, the exactest possible copy, and yet it has neither motion nor eloquence. Art intervenes to exaggerate certain surfaces, and also to fine down others. In sculpture everything depends upon the way in which the modelling is carried out with a constant thought of the main line of the scheme, upon the rendering of the hollows, of the projections and of their connections; thus it is that one may get fine lights, and especially fine shadows that are not opaque. Everything should be emphasised according to the accent that it is desired to render, and the degree of amplification is personal, according to the tact and the temperament of each sculptor; and for this reason there is no transmissible process, no studio recipe, but only a true law. I see it in the antique and in Michelangelo. To work by the profiles, in depth not by surfaces, always thinking of the few geometrical forms from which all nature proceeds, and to make these eternal forms perceptible in the individual case of the object studied, that is my criterion. That is not idealism, it is a part of the handicraft. My ideas have nothing to do with it but for that method; my Danaids and my Dante figures would be weak, bad things. From the large design that I get your mind deduces ideas."

Rodin, then, is convinced that he is classical, and rebels

against the "École" which claims to be so. He has the greatest admiration for the Renascence, but declares that he does not so clearly understand the genius of the Gothic sculptors. He admires it, but has not thoroughly penetrated it. "I feel it, but I cannot express it," he says. "I cannot analyse the Celtic genius to my own satisfaction. In the Middle Ages art came from groups, not from individuals. It was anonymous; the sculptors of cathedrals no more put their names to their works than our workmen put theirs on the pavement that they lay. Ah! what an admirable scorn of notoriety! The signature is what destroys us. We do portraits, but what we do is not so great. These kings and queens, on the cathedrals, were not portraits. The fellow-workers stood for one another, and they interpreted; they did not copy. They made clothed figures; the nude and portraiture only date from the Renascence. And then those fellows cut with the tool's end into the block, that is why they were called sculptors. As for us, we are modellers. And what a disgraceful thing that casting from life is, which so many well-known sculptors do not blush to use! It is a mere swindling in art. Art was a vital function to the image-makers of the thirteenth century; they would have laughed at the idea of signing what they did, and never dreamed of honours and titles. When once their work was finished, they said no more about it, or else they talked among themselves. How curious it would have been to hear them, to be present at their gatherings, where they must have discussed in amusing phrases, and with simple, deep ideas!... Whenever the cathedrals disappear civilisation will go down one step. And even now we no longer understand them, we no longer know how to read their silent language. *We need to make excavations not in the earth, but towards heaven....*" An admirable saying that Rodin has often repeated to me and that I have never heard without deep emotion! He has the secret of these true formulas, and his words, which are not eloquent, but, rather, obscure, are suddenly lighted up by them. His speech, like his sculpture, is born from sincere contact with the essence of nature. In regard to the Renascence and

Michelangelo, he reports that he received no decisive lesson from either until after a journey to Italy in 1875. "I believed before that," he says,

> "that movement was the whole secret of this art, and I put my models into positions like those of Michelangelo. But as I went on observing the free attitudes of my models I perceived that they possessed these *naturally,* and that Michelangelo had not preconceived them, but merely transcribed them according to the personal inspiration of human beings moved by the need of action. I went to Rome to look for what may be found everywhere: *the latent heroic in every natural movement.* [*4]
>
> "Then I gathered the elements of what people call my symbolism. I do not understand anything about long words and theories. But I am willing to be a symbolist, if that defines the ideas that Michelangelo gave me, namely that the essence of sculpture is the modelling, the general scheme which alone enables us to render the intensity, the supple variety of movement and character. If we can imagine the thought of God in creating the world, He thought first of the construction, which is the sole principle of nature, of living things and perhaps of the planets. Michelangelo seems to me rather to derive from Donatello than from the ancients; Raphael proceeds from them. He understood that an architecture can be built up with the human body, and that, in order to possess volume and harmony, a statue or a group ought to be contained in a cube, a pyramid; or some simple figure. Let us look at a Dutch interior and at an interior painted by an artist of the present day. The latter no longer touches us, because it does not possess the qualities of depth and volume, the science of distances. The artist who paints it does not know how to reproduce a cube. An interior by Van der Meer is a cubic painting. The atmosphere is in it and the exact volume of the objects; the place of these objects has been respected, the modern painter places them, arranges them as models. The Dutchmen did not touch them, but set themselves to render the distances that separated them, that is, the depth. And then, if I go so far as to say that *cubic truth, not appearance, is the mistress of things,* if I add that the sight of the plains and woods and country views gives me the principle of the plans that I employ on my statues, that I feel cubic truth everywhere, and that plan and volume appear to me as laws of all life and all beauty, will it be said that I am a symbolist, that I generalise, that I am a metaphysician? It seems to me that I have remained a sculptor and a realist. Unity oppresses and haunts me."

"What," says Rodin again,

"is the principle of my figures, and what is it that people like in them? It is the very pivot of art, it is balance; that is to say, the oppositions of volume produced by movement. That is the striking, material fact in art, with all due deference to those persons who conceive art as distinct from 'brutal' reality. Art is like love. For many people it is a dream, a psychological complication, a palace, a perfume, a stage scene; but nothing of the sort! The essential of love is the pairing; all the rest is only detail, charming, and full of passion, but detail. It is the same in art: people come and praise my symbols and my expressions to me; but I know that the plans are the essential thing. Respect the plan, make it exact from every point; movement intervenes, displaces these volumes and creates a fresh balance. The human body is like a *walking temple,* and like a temple it has a central point around which the volumes place and spread themselves. When one understands that, one has everything. It is simple, but it must be seen, and academism refuses to see it. Instead of recognising that that is the key to my method they prefer to say that I am a poet. That expression signifies that people feel, confusedly, the difference between an art resting on conventions and one derived from truth; only they think that the 'poetic' art is the conventional one. They call that *inspiration.* That is the belief that has led to the theory of genius being madness. But men of genius are just those*who, by their trade-skill, carry the essential thing to perfection.* People say that my sculpture *is that of an 'exalté.'*[*5]
    "I do not deny that there is exaltation in my works; but that exaltation existed not in me, but in nature, in movement. The divine work is naturally exalted. As for me, all I do is to be true; my temperament is not 'exalted'; it is patient. I am not a dreamer, but a mathematician; and if my sculpture is good it is because it is geometrical."

From these fragments of conversation the reader will conceive how Rodin's generalising spirit leads him from the realism of his daily work to the synthesis of a sort of ideo-realistic metaphysical system. He has the sense (belonging only to genius) of the *continuity of the universe,* and he certainly had it at a time when, unlettered as he was, he would not have known how to explain it specifically to himself. He constantly formulates this metaphysical system, as I have seen it formulated by Stéphane Mallarmé, who could never see anything without instantly bringing together two ideas or images that no one would ever have thought of connecting. Spontaneous analogy is the mark of genius and the secret of all real poetry. This is why I consider Rodin as a very great poet – not in the sense that he dislikes, but on the contrary, by giving to the word "poet" its deep etymological significance according to the Greek, that of "making, creating, vivifying." We may understand, too, in how great a degree an intellectuality of this kind offers a living challenge to the ideas of the "École." The man who thinks thus is necessarily isolated and has struggled all his life, never making a concession and saying nobly, "The artist, like the woman, has an honour to preserve." I will further quote from Rodin the following reflection[*6]: "Where you follow nature, you get everything. When I have a beautiful woman's body for a model the drawings that I make from it give me images of insects, birds, and fishes. That seems improbable, and I had no suspicion of it myself. Formerly I used to be seeking shapes for vases, either to use them at Sèvres, where I used to work, or elsewhere.... I never succeeding in finding a beauty of proportions and lines such as I had the feeling of, because I only founded my attempts upon *imagination*. Since that time I have drawn women's bodies, and one of these bodies gave me, in the synthesis of it, a magnificent shape for a vase, with true and harmonious lines. The point is not to create. Creation and improvisation are useless words. Genius only comes to the man who understands with his eye and his brain. Everything is in the things about us. Manufacture and ornamental art want reforming according to these ideas. I should have liked to see that. Everything-is contained in nature. There is an harmonious, continual, uninterrupted movement. A woman, a mountain, a horse, in conception they are all the same thing, they are made on the same principles. Young artists compose instead of following their models and understanding that therein lies infinity." Here Rodin directly touches a scientific truth – the relative monotony of Nature's productive forms. Nature does everything with very few forms: the variations are so infinite that there are no two leaves alike, but the nerves of a leaf, the lines of a vein, an artery, a bird's wing, a fishbone, a nerve-cell, are identical; multiplicity derives from identity and returns to it, so that everything is reduced to a fundamental geometry which perhaps is but the effect of a single cellular generation. In this respect the laws of art and of science are the same, even as among all the arts there is a synthesis of common laws, an identity where we seem to behold a difference. Recent work in science, by establishing the existence of states of radiation (Crookes, Röntgen, Hertz) is busy undermining our old conception of matter, showing us the identity of it with the immaterial, and thereby abolishing our preconceptions about the idea and the fact, music and sculpture, considered as different manifestations. I remember that I one day kept Rodin's curiosity excited for a long time by explaining the details of this theory to him; he was not acquainted with it, and listened to me as to a writer in love with general ideas. But it was clear that in his mere province as a sculptor he knew far better and had penetrated far more deeply into this enthralling problem of identity. His is a luminous mind, of the same kind as the electric rays; it rather penetrates than surrounds what is obscure to it. On that day he was disturbed, and I was irritated by certain declamations which had been written about his "philosophy," and of which the author had assuredly not comprehended the logical consequences; and we came to the conclusion that it would be much better for Rodin's peace of mind to keep silent upon these points, for his "philosophy" could only be made comprehensible to those who could understand the method of his sculpture.

It is time, however, to pause in this path and to return simply to the question of sculpture. Nor was it my purpose to tire the reader by these abstractions when I began to say a few words about Rodin's opinions concerning the antique. It must be understood, then, that the *Balzac* and even the *Hugo*, as well as some figures, were the result of all these preceding reflections. "When I saw my *Balzac* brought into the yard from the storehouse of the statues in order to go to the Salon," says Rodin, "I had it purposely placed beside *The Kiss,* which had been finished rather earlier. I was not dissatisfied with the simplified vigour of that group, to which I had already applied these experiments. But I saw that it looked slack, that it did not hold its place beside the *Balzac* as Michelangelo's torso does beside a fine antique, and then I understood that I was in the right path. I have had hesitations, you know, pangs that I do not speak of. And then, little by little, as I looked at nature, as I came to understand it better and to throw aside my prejudices more frankly, I took courage. It seemed to me that I was doing better. When I began I did skilful things, things that were smartly done, but they were thin and dry, but I felt there was something beyond, and that something is amplification. I only ventured on it when I was over fifty years old, but do you not think I have a right now to disregard the objections of the mob and the newspapers? I have taken time to know why I was doing as I did. The essential things of my modelling are there, and they would be there in less degree if I 'finished' more. As to polishing or repolishing a toe or a curl, I find no interest in it; it impairs the large line, the soul of what I desired to do, and I have nothing more to say to the public on that point. There the line of demarcation comes between the confidence that the public ought to have in me and the concessions that I ought not to make to the public." To this firm and discreet resolution Rodin has kept in all the works wrought out by him since 1898.

I cannot better set forth his opinions about the antique than by quoting the following fragments from two articles that he wrote for the *Musée,* a review of ancient art, in January and February, 1904; for Rodin sometimes writes, quite unpretentiously, but with the same lucidity of thought that he shows in his familiar conversation. One of these articles refers to a Greek statuette in the Museum of Naples, the other to the lesson that the ancients give us.

"In the first place, the Antique is Life itself. Nothing is more alive, and no style in the world has rendered life as it has. The ancients were the greatest, most serious, and most admirable observers of nature who have ever existed. The antique was able to render life because the ancients saw the essential thing in it – large blocks. They confined themselves to the large shadows cast by these large blocks, and as truth itself lies in that, their figures being so made could never be feeble. Moreover, the antique is simple, and that gives it astonishing energy. And then there is much more study in it than appears; that was brought home to me once. When I had finished my *Age of Brass*, I went to Italy and I found an Apollo whose leg was in exactly the same position as one in *The Age of Brass* that had taken me six months' work. Then I saw that though on the surface everything seems to be done at a stroke, in reality all the muscles are built up and one sees the details come to light one by one. That is because the ancients studied everything in its successive profiles, because in any figure and every part of a figure no profile is like another; when each has been studied separately the whole appears simple and alive.

"The great error of the neo-Greek school is really this: it is not *type* that is antique, but modelling. For want of having understood that, the neo-Greek school has produced nothing but papier-mâché. It is bad to put the antique before beginners; one should end, not begin with it. If you wanted to teach someone to eat, you would give him fresh food, that he might learn to chew; it would never occur to you to give him food already triturated to exercise his teeth upon. Well, when you want to teach sculpture to anyone, set him face to face with nature, and when he has gained plenty of power to deal with nature, then say to him: 'Now, here is what the antique has done.' And that will give him a new source of energy. Whereas if you give the antique to the beginner who has never struggled with nature, he does not understand anything about it, and loses his individuality over it. You make a plagiarist of him, and instead of making his own prayer to nature he will repeat the prayer of the antique without understanding the words of it. He will die an old pupil; he will not die a man.

"To teach the antique at the outset of a man's studies is to render the antique incomprehensible. In the first place, no one can teach the antique, it is not possible; that art of truth and simplicity cannot be taught. The sculptor works from nature, and afterwards he goes to look, in the galleries, and see how the antique rendered what he has been trying for from the life. But if he goes straight to the antique, shutting his eyes to nature, as the antique has always been done from nature, our sculptor will only be able to carry that vision into his own work in a factitious way; he will be neither antique nor modern, but bad.

"A man may do antique work in our day, not in the false sense of producing the *antique type*, but in the true sense of *modelling like the antique*. Such a man (painter, etcher, or sculptor) will take nature, and if he has the power of the antique he will produce antique work, which will entirely disagree with what is taught as such, but will agree with that in the museums. The 'École' begins at the end; when a man begins with nature, he may go on to the most improbable inventions; the antiques themselves show that. Do you know of anything more impossible than the centaur? But is there anything finer in Olympia? The ancients knew nature so well that they became her fellow-workers and created, not phantoms, but beings that were alive in spite of physical impossibilities. To my mind it would be better not to study the antique than to study it wrong. It is not the artist's alphabet, but the reward of his work. The command which it gives us is not to copy it, but to do like it.

"To say that the antiques, which portray the plain marvel of life, are beautiful is a superficial sort of praise. Beauty is not the starting-point, but the point of arrival; a thing can only be beautiful if it is true. Truth itself is only a complete harmony, and harmony is finally only a bundle of utilities. The miracle of life could not be perpetuated but for the constant renewal of universal balance. The ancients felt that vast rhythm, and their art, being modelled upon it, appears to us as a natural and sublime expression of beauty…. One of the ancients made a statue. How did he set about it? It is useless to bring in rules that only grew up in the brains of commentators dissecting a series of works, centuries afterwards. The antique remains uncomprehended because we have not a simple enough spirit. It is not by studying the antique that we shall learn its secret; in order to understand, not its nomenclature, but its spirit, we must begin by studying nature. Rembrandt cannot be understood by copying him at the Louvre, he can only be understood when we travel through nature to him. Well, nature is always there, waiting patiently for antiques to be made afresh; the model is there waiting for someone to come at last, no matter whence. For it is an error to think the antique comes from the south: it comes from everywhere. The antique can be produced from a Dutch woman or an American woman; the type is nothing, the modelling is everything.

"What makes the strength of the antique is the plan, the connection of all the profiles. The neo-Greeks say: 'The antiques are *line*, and their works, in which all the lines, except two, dance about, show their error. The antiques, we will say, are *lines* or rather *plan*. Look at an antique; you can guess the full face from the profile. The eye cannot grasp the shape on the opposite side to that which it beholds, but it deduces it from this side: walk round, and the study of the profiles will afford you an *irrefragable* proof by *rule of three*. The sculptor swells the half-tones by slight exaggerations, so as to heighten the light by a tone. The drapery lives; like the body that it hides, it receives life from that body without needing the subterfuge of wetted drapery.'[*7]

"There is in the antiques an astonishing mystery of life which causes all idea of dimension to disappear. A figure an inch or two high might just as well be life-size; when a thing is well organised, the greatness is in the modelling and not in the size. If one were to photograph a Tanagra figure and the Eiffel Tower, and were to show the two photographs to some person unacquainted with either object, I am sure he would declare the Tanagra figure to be larger than the tower. A pear or an apple, from the point of view of modelling, is as large as the celestial sphere. Thus the splendour of truth is such that finding no word to render it, we have called it 'Ideal.'"

These quotations will suffice, I hope, to show Rodin's inmost thought. These judgments are implicit condemnations of the "École"; they are also definitions of his classical art, which is by no means "literary," and which is governed, even in its lyrical and tragic developments, by good sense, that is to say, by an inborn taste for balance in the midst of boldness. If I am anxious to insist so strongly upon Rodin's profound *normality*, this is, I repeat, in order to forewarn the public against the declamations of some of his untoward admirers, who reckon one of his merits to be an "originality" which they confound with that exaggeration, that emphasis and eccentricity that never mark the great artist. Whatever tragic or passionate subject a great artist may treat, to whatever height of strangeness his imagination may rise, beauty of form will, if he is, like Rodin, a master of *technique*, confer upon t him an exalted and permanent serenity. Rembrandt and Delacroix come from the depth of their vastly differing worlds to meet Raphael and Watteau in that conciliatory region where we admire the great masters – and Rodin is already placed in that region.

IV

WORKS SINCE THE "BALZAC" – SMALL WORKS IN
MARBLE – PLAN OF THE MONUMENT TO LABOUR –
DRAWINGS AND ETCHINGS

"I shun father and mother and wife and brother, when my genius
calls me. I would write on the lintels of the door-post, *Whim.* I hope it
is somewhat better than whim at last, but we cannot spend the day in
explanation…. Whoso would be a man must be a nonconformist …
must not be hindered by the name of goodness, but must inquire if it
be goodness. Nothing is at last sacred but the integrity of our own
mind. Absolve you to yourself, and you shall have the suffrage of the
world."

I quoted these high-minded words of Emerson's to Rodin at the
time of the *Balzac* incident. "They are," I said to him, "the very
epigraph of your whole life." Nor have they ceased to epitomise
the man and the artist. From the time of the *Balzac* Rodin's work
has proceeded very regularly and on the same principles. The
Victor Hugo is being finished in marble, in its two versions, in the
studio of the Rue de l'Université. The group in which Hugo, his
extended arm commanding silence of the waves, sits surrounded
by Muses is almost ready; the other, in which Hugo, dreamily
listening to the counsels of Iris, stands on the edge of a rock
washed by waves, amid which Nereids are entwined, is not quite
so far advanced. *The Gate of Hell* is ready to receive its finally

chosen and ordered figures. In the Salon of 1902 Rodin exhibited the three *Shades* from its summit, inspired by the celebrated *Lasciate ogni speransa*. In 1900 Rodin only showed two or three old productions at the Universal Exhibition, because his work was collected in a special pavilion at the Rond-point de l'Alma, the concession of which pavilion was made uncomfortable for him by his colleagues, so much so that the artist was obliged to remove on the very day of closing, with less delay and consideration allowed to him than to the most unimportant industrial exhibitor. This special exhibition was, nevertheless, a great international success for Rodin, and the amazing development of his fame may be said to date from it. Before 1900 Rodin stood in the position of an exceptional artist, celebrated but envied, isolated and challenged, whose relations with the Government were strained, whom a minority upheld, but on whom the official world looked coldly. Since that time his eminence is so firmly established that he now holds the rank that Puvis de Chavannes held in the estimation of all artists. His triumphant journey to Prague (1901-2), London's enthusiastic reception, and Rodin's recent election to be President of the Society over which Whistler presided, have finally given him the acknowledgment so long looked for. In 1903 his marble bust of Hugo aroused enthusiasm, and at the Salon of 1904 the colossal bronze *Thinker* had a most flattering reception, and disarmed the last of his former detractors.

A woman's bust accompanied *The Thinker* to the Salon. Rodin, who does portraits now and again, had previously made an admirable one of Mme. Fenaille, wife of the art-patron who had been of such great service to him; and he is attempting a curious variation of it. He has just finished a bust of a helmeted Minerva, as impressive as a Donatello, and this, too, is a portrait.

Various works have been produced by Rodin since the *Balzac*, in addition to the *Monument of President Sarmiento*, which shows an admirable bas-relief of a radiant Apollo. These works are nearly all in marble, and small. It is almost impossible to describe and classify them; a much larger book would be required, and my main purpose here has been to give a general idea of Rodin's art and an explanation of principles. I have spoken about some of his poems of the flesh, especially that *Eternal Idol*, which will be the glory of thought in modern sculpture. Rodin's recent works in marble have the same inspiration. Some demand special notice: *The Hand of God*, a gigantic hand, between the fingers of which, and amid a handful of clay, two beings are tenderly embracing; *Icarus*, falling from the sky to be crushed on the earth amid his whirling wings; several groups of lovers, entwined, and breathing immeasurable tenderness, the most celebrated of which is *Spring* or *Love and Psyche*. Another *Psyche*, alone, is discovering Love asleep, with extraordinary restrained emotion; and there are several attempts at *Poets and Muses*, embracing or consoling one another, as well as a splendid sketch of the *Magdalen wiping Christ's Body with her Hair*. Rodin has thus sometimes touched religious subjects, but with an undogmatic symbolism, philosophic and wide. We may also enumerate another version in marble of the *Nereids* of the Hugo monument, a winged *Inspiration* coming to breathe upon the sleeping poet, and holding back the tips of her wings with one hand lest she should make a sound in closing them; a faun drawing towards him a nymph, who struggles in silent, fierce resistance; two high-reliefs of *Summer* and *Autumn* in stone; tall women with children, intended for the town of Evian, where Baron Vitta is accumulating treasures of modern art; *Pygmalion* beholding his statue come to life, who, as soon as she feels herself live, turns from him with a surprising movement of coquetry and aversion. Such works as these cannot be described in words. In them Rodin has excelled to an unparalleled degree in rendering the profoundest psychological complexities, refined intentions, and the hesitations of feeling. I will further note a sketch of *Sappho*, seated at rest, with her arms leaning upon two little naked women, which is a work inspired equally by the Greeks and by the eighteenth century; it bears witness to the artist's wish of avoiding the massive, and making as many holes as possible within the general block, so as to give lightness and to allow a circulation of light, as the Greeks did in works that were meant to stand against a background of sea or of sky. Many studies of men and women crouching, or squatting, in curious attitudes, recall the art of the Japanese bronzes, which Rodin immensely admires. We must further note some groups of *Women Damned,* in which Rodin's art attains the highest point of voluptuous tension, audacious suggestiveness, and tragic eagerness of the flesh aspiring to impossible delight. This whole world of figures is ruled by the same lyrical and poetic imagination, the same symbolism incarnated in impeccable forms. Everywhere we find the same nervous art, agitating, sad, and ardent in its voluptuous character, expressing the insatiability of human souls; the aspiration of a troubled time towards an ideality which would deliver it from the solicitations of pessimism; the hope of escape by the way of desire; and love sought for in the over-excitement of neurosis. Rodin, gloomy psychologist of passion, understands the disease of the age, and at the same time pities it; a true thinker, he extracts its mournful beauty without ceasing to retain faith, admiration, and affection for the human creature. Bending over life and over his work, he is himself his own *Thinker,* attentive and reverent before an unknown and terrible divinity. Never did any other sculptor attempt to vivify his art with such intellectual superiority and by such meditations, and Rodin is at once the most realistic and most metaphysical of poets in stone and bronze.

Two or three works of more important dimensions stand out from his recent productions; besides a nude female torso (in bronze) of startling truthfulness, and two plaster studies that astonished at the Salons, and besides *The Christian Martyr,* so masterly in its modelling, Rodin has continued to work at his *Ugolino,* taken out of *The Gate of Hell,* and has put the finishing touch to two plans. One of these is the *Monument to Labour,* a grand conception, which one may dream of seeing carried out and rising up in some square of busy Paris, but which want of money will prevent from ever being realised. It is a column upon a vast rectangular base, with a crypt in it. Two colossal figures of *Night* and *Day* would stand at the entrance. In the crypt would be shown, in bas-relief, different subterranean works – mining, etc. Around the column would run a covered spiral staircase, and upon the column itself would be figured in bas-reliefs all the various manifestations of labour, so that as one ascended the stairs all the divers phases of human genius could be successively studied. On the top would hover the *Benedictions*, two – winged spirits, descended from heaven, which are already executed in marble on a small scale, and are among Rodin's finest conceptions. This colossal project was conceived as long ago as 1897. The rough model is in the studio at Meudon-Val-Fleury.

The monument to Puvis de Chavannes was entrusted to his friend Rodin, and is already finished. Rodin conceived it in an original and charming way. Instead of making the customary statue, he considered the purely Greek quality of Puvis' genius and chose to pay homage to him in a form reproduced from the antique. The bust of the great painter is placed on a plain table, as the ancients placed those of their dead upon little domestic altars. A fine tree loaded with fruit bends over and shades the head. Leaning on the table behind the bust is a beautiful naked youth, who sits dreaming in a well-chosen supple attitude. The whole design is intimate, gentle, and pure. Placed on the ground in a garden this votive monument would show how much delicacy and caressing lightness sometimes lies in Rodin's sombre and pathetic thoughts.

Another important group is that of *Orpheus and Eurydice*. Orpheus has fallen on one knee and is lifting his great lyre towards the gods whom he has just implored. Above him, almost on his back, suspended in a way that would appear to contradict the laws of equilibrium and the material conditions of sculpture, soars Eurydice, compassionate and almost vaporous, truly an immaterial shade, with a smile of despair. I regret that the unfinished condition of this model does not allow me to publish a photograph of it, for nothing would give a clearer impression of

Rodin's originality in the matter of contour and in the mutual relation of figures. The extreme freedom of his attitudes and his caprices of balance are, indeed, the newest features that he has brought into his art and are not to be found in anyone else in any country or time. In these is his true signature, and by them his work might be recognised among a hundred statues of all periods. As to the expressive beauty of the faces and bodies, that is supreme. No one has better comprehended than Rodin all that can be rendered by the naked human body and all the intellectual significations that it can hide. The nude is to Rodin a whole language.

In his latest spiritualised works there is something Correggio-like in the vibration of light upon the softened forms and amplified surfaces. They suggest the *Antiope,* at once soft and muscular, and Rodin often speaks of "morbidezza" as a quality which he no longer distrusts, whereas he formerly banished it from his ascetic, sinewy, and dry figures. He gives his women the pulpy flesh of fruits. The lines of landscape seem to him to correspond to the planes of the body; he lately said to me that since he has lived at Meudon, opposite the flowing Seine, the wooded hills and the fields, he has found useful resemblances between the modelling of the body and that of a horizon. I have even once suggested to him the title of "The Hill" for the body of a young man reclining, the outline of which did in truth resemble the undulations of a hill, and he retained the name and the analogy, for he delights in everything that binds the human being to the earth, and, like a true metaphysician, conceives of nothing isolated or distinct in nature.

I come now to Rodin's drawings, drawings which were not made to be shown, but which, having nevertheless become known, have surprised and puzzled people. Rodin's drawings, like some other drawings by sculptors, are not themselves works of art; they are thoughts noted down, and are not comprehensible unless they are seen with the statues of which they indicate the first idea, or some variation.

Rodin has published some of his sketches; and has produced some dry-points (in particular the *Ronde*,[*1] *Antonin Proust*, the three portraits of Henry Becque, full face and two profiles upon the same sheet, and two heads of Hugo), some drawings for books by M. Mirbeau and M. Bergerat, and a complete set of illustrations of the *Fleurs du Mal*, in the form of marginal drawings for a unique copy belonging to M. Gallimard. Many drawings in black or colour have been published (by the clever lithographer Clot), and M. Fenaille has superintended an admirable *edition de luxe* of 142 drawings by Rodin.[*2] Notwithstanding this partial publicity, these works must be considered as *standing apart;* and to consider them by themselves would actually be to injure Rodin with the public at large, since they form an integral part of his statues. For this reason I have not chosen to reproduce any of them here, studies so purely professional not seeming to fall within the scope of a work intended to give a general idea of an artist's work.

Having said so much, I wish to dwell upon the great beauty of these drawings – a special and terrible beauty. Many deal with Dante. Rodin did some painting under Lecoq de Boisbaudron, landscapes, a portrait of his father, and sketches after Rubens; but there has never been any danger of painting intruding upon his vocation, and his sketches rapidly became nothing but notes for sculpture. The objective reality of his Dantesque figures is vague, if their subjective reality is intense. Rodin, anxious to note down his impressions, and not to *illustrate*, made his sketches into a sort of passionate writing, only devoting himself to the scheme and to the contrasts of black and white, and neglecting every detail. In these violent washes, these pencillings and pen-scribbles, the spectator who is not forewarned sees nothing, but the lover of art, who knows beforehand what to seek, follows the creative thought. Nothing can be less like what is generally known as "a drawing." After the regular drawings, the "painter's drawings" of his first period, which have but a restricted interest, and which are no longer known, those of his second manner are confusions of light and shadow, and show fantastically. I will quote at this point a passage from an essay by M. Clément Jasmin, a discerning critic, whose noisy rivals do not give him his due place, and who has described these works excellently.

"These sketches are altogether the work of a sculptor, even in their colour, which seems to have sunk into plaster or clay, and especially in the firmness of their modelling, which is imparted by shaded touches of body-colour, on grey paper, or rendered by spaces left white. These blanks, these white spaces, are the extreme point of the modelling, the 'high light' of some projection, which lower down is wrapped in half-tints that carry the eye to the shadows of the inflections or the hollows. There is a constant relation between the contour and the interior modelling. A thrill is communicated by the fantastic lighting of some sketches. Rodin adds further strength to this dramatic distribution of lights and shadows by one or two tones that accentuate the impression or fix a plan. Often his ink will become blue or yellow, (water-colours, sepia, or coloured inks being employed), in order to settle a value or intensify a feeling. Such is the case in the Fenaille publication, with the gloomy red in the face of the Ugolino, of the Dantesque Mahomet, whose entrails are hanging out, and of some other figures dashed in, in black, on a violet background. One plainly feels the material in which the work, of which the sketch is the first idea, will be executed. It is always a sculptor who is at work, even when he exchanges the chisel for the pen or the brush."

Painters would scorn these drawings. They commonly believe that sculptors cannot express upon a plane surface the mass and movement of a body. In reality a painter's sketch and a sculptor's sketch differ in intention and execution. Rodin's are translations of movements, in no way decorative and not attempting to express either modelling or detail, but, if we may say so, the abstract geometry, the thought that commands the movement. The use of coloured inks, which are solely meant to modify certain values that black or white would not express to Rodin's mind, has given rise to mistakes. These colours are not there to express real tints, as is the case in ordinary drawings thus touched up; inaccurate things have been said about these colourings, and about the fantastic and almost Japanese appearance of some of the plates.

Rodin is certainly not thinking of prints in colour. He makes these notes instinctively, and displays not so much a deliberate thought as a natural faculty of transcription.

In his early drawings Rodin *refers to* – for I must insist upon the point that the drawings do not *represent* things – many of Dante's persons and many fanciful animals, and later, to his statues. Now he does not draw at all from literary impressions, but solely from the living model. He uses ordinary cheap paper, a pencil or a pen; he makes his model take some transitory, absolutely free position, often in the rest between two sittings, and rapidly draws contour without taking his eyes from the model and without looking at his sketch. Sometimes the stroke will fall upon emptiness, the sheet of paper will be too small, a head or a limb will fail to find its place. Naturally this instantaneous sketch will be deformed in the most unexpected way; the proportions are false, but the scheme of the contour and the modelling of each piece are true. Often the hurrying pencil will miss the curve of a breast or a leg. Then the artist will return to that point with hasty, intermingled, impatient strokes that play around the true line. His only concern is to fix the first view, the absolutely living impression. Afterwards, in tracing his sketch, he rectifies, but his chief aim is to amplify the impression of the life, taken spontaneously, according to his principle of enlarging the form, in order to place it better in the atmosphere (about in the proportion of 5/4 instead of 4/4). Then he connects the contours and further enlarges the modelling, filling the outline with a wash of burnt-sienna, which gives the general value, or sometimes with blue or red water-colour. Rodin likes this practice in catching movements, and he has in his studio hundreds of drawings of this kind that differ from his early ones. Those aimed at the imaginative transcription of tragic and literary elements under strange illuminations, and were almost like the drawings of Odilon Redon; the later ones are merely graphic notes of movements, and are incapable of having any direct aim or meaning.

I must add a few words upon a delicate point of which I

should not have spoken if others had not spoken mistakenly upon the subject. Rodin's drawings, especially those of the present time, have shocked some people who have seen them by their licentious character. Why should we assume embarrassment in explaining this? In all Rodin's work there is a profound and violent sense of the voluptuous, and the stern painter of the vices and damnations of hell does not need to think of prudery. The elevation and dramatic character of his conceptions clothe the most daring attitudes with the severe chastity of the beautiful. In his sketches, made for himself alone, and in the privacy of his studio, Rodin no more fears erotic positions than did Hokusai. Beneath the original animality he perceives nature; and feminine sexuality, its movements, and impulses interest him, because therein woman is psychologically revealed. Everything, in physical desire, that exalts, maddens, contorts, and fevers the human body is, for the sculptor, the object of an intensely interested study that he does not communicate to the general public; nor is he the only one among the great artists of form whom the erotic has interested from this point of view. Only mediocre minds and minds capable of low intentions see anything low in the movements of life. Rodin's studies from the model, naked and free, without spectators, in the serious presence of work, never sully his grand and melancholy inspiration; and his daring art is assuredly that which most leads away the beholder from erotic ideas, because it notes in every human being the melancholy of the insatiable, and makes the pleasure of the senses a suffering of the flesh and the spirit. By this point he touches the profound morality of art, and his consciousness is free from any equivocation. The recent drawings in which he catches the animal attitudes of the model are thus no more questionable, from the delicate point of view of which I am speaking, than anatomical plates, or the sad immodesties of a post-mortem examination. He adds to them the power of expressing passion with which he is endowed, but since he only shows these drawings to friends and artists in whom nudity does not arouse silly thoughts, this concerns no one else. A comparison cannot even be ventured between these drawings and the masterly etchings of Rops, which are deliberate illustrations of licentious subjects, relieved only by beauty of execution, and which should only be shown with express reservations. Rodin admires certain bronzes in the secret museum at Naples, and certain Japanese prints, because in these, too, art has done its work by expressing a secret and essential spring of the nervous and psychological life of humanity; a fierce and serious subject which only fools consider laughable or indecent, because their minds approach it with indecorum and ridicule. But I do not know that Rodin ever even yielded to the fancy of modelling one of these subjects for himself, as Rubens and many others did not forbid themselves to do. It is time, therefore, to have done with this question in regard to the great French sculptor. I do not know for whom he intends these recent drawings, a whole framed collection of which occupies one of the storerooms of his country house. Perhaps he will have them destroyed; in any case, they are but studies of movements and masses, and in no way direct representations of life.

Rodin's drawings are "rough drafts" to be compared with those of a writer. Some are very impressive, and all constitute precious evidence of his psychological preoccupations and of his desire for simplification. But they remain on the margin of his work, and neither the public nor the critics have those rights over them that belong to biographers and friends. That is a point to be plainly specified, and I desire to repeat that that is the reason this book contains none of them.

V

RODIN'S PRIVATE LIFE – HIS PERSON, STUDIO, AND HOME – HIS INFLUENCE; SCULPTORS INSPIRED BY HIS IDEAS – RODIN'S PLACE IN THE FRENCH SCHOOL – HIS PRESENT POSITION IN RESPECT TO ACADEMIC SCULPTURE

Auguste Rodin is in person a man of middle height, with an enormous head upon a massive torso. At first sight one sees nothing of him but this leonine bust, the head with its strong nose, flowing grey beard, and small, keen, light-coloured eyes, slightly veiled by short sight and by a gentle irony. The impression of power is accentuated by the rolling gait, the rocky aspect of the troubled brow under the rough brush of hair, the bony thickness of the aquiline nose and the ample curls of beard. But the first impression is partly contradicted by the reticent line of the mouth, the quick look, penetrating, simple, and arch, (one of the most composite glances I have ever seen), and especially by the voice, which is hollow, not easily modulated, with deep inflections and sudden returns to a dental pronunciation, and of which the meaning and intention are further modified by certain very expressive tossings of the head. He appears simple, precise, reserved, courteous, and cordial, without liveliness. Little by little his shyness gives place to a calm and remarkable tone of authority. He is neither emphatic nor awkward, and would seem rather dispirited than inspired. An immense energy breathes in his sober and measured gestures. The slowness and apparent embarrassment of his speech and the pauses in his conversation give especial significance to what he says; moreover, Rodin has acquired of late years a genuine case as a talker and even as a writer, which previously he did not possess. I was intimately acquainted with Stéphane Mallarmé, who, measured by Rodin, was incomparably eloquent, and I often associate these two men in my thoughts. The voices were alike, and Rodin, too, with his improvised phrases, has the same veiled circumspect way of speech, hitting suddenly upon words that illuminate the idea.

Rodin, in speaking of any work of his, has a way of explaining it that is very elliptical, but very clear, and which has caused some brilliant chatterers to say, because he did not offer a prolix commentary, that he did not know what he had done. In reality he utters the essential, and his gesture, which seems to model his thought in space, completes his words. He looks lovingly on his creations, and sometimes seems to meditate in astonishment at the idea of having created them; he speaks of them as though they existed apart from himself.

Gradually, beneath Rodin's essential simplicity, one discovers features that were at first hidden; he is ironical, sensuous, nervous, proud. He contains as possibilities all the passions that he expresses with so vibrating a magnificence, and one begins to perceive the secret links between this calm, almost cheerful man and the art that he reveals. At certain moments his clear and rather vague eyes become full of phosphorescent points, the face grows sardonic and almost faunlike; at others it saddens and discloses a sickness for infinity. This man is the comrade of his dumb white creatures; he loves them, follows their abstract life, has moral obligations towards them. Fundamentally the one thing with which Rodin is really concerned is the life of permanent forms. Of late celebrity, age, and experience have disposed him to become an adviser, a master, and he has begun to talk æsthetics. But his ideas and opinions are restricted. He perceives human beings only very summarily, his cordiality is a way of fulfilling his social duties hastily. He has, if I may venture the expression, very fine moral antennae, and they serve to recognise the persons whom he will like. Very capable of friendship, Rodin reduces friendship to tacit agreements upon the essential subjects of thought, and it is only if one meets him upon one of these points that one takes a place in his remembrance or his liking. He does not put his faith in individuals, but in general ideas. He loves nothing but his work, and endures everything else with civil boredom. He has a horror of debates and disturbances. I have never heard him speak ill of bad artists; he neglects, but does not criticise. He has a silent humour which leads him to make busts of official and mediocre sculptors, with an amusing good grace. Uncompromising in everything that touches his art, Rodin has throughout his whole career endured severe struggles and grave injustices, and, too proud to dispute, has never shown his secret revolts. At the time when the *Balzac* was refused all Rodin's friends said to him: "Resist, force your work upon them; you ought, for the work's sake, and a court would surely decide for you, for your agreement is definitely in your favour." He listened and thanked them, always good-tempered, and then withdrew his statue without saying anything.

It is not weakness, for Rodin has had an excessively hard life and is strong and patient; it is dignity of the inner life and profound indifference for the life about him. Rodin is a high dignitary of the Legion of Honour, a president of the judges of sculpture of an important society of artists (the Société Nationale), he is honoured all over Europe, has been received in England as a genius, and has succeeded Whistler as the head of a chosen band of artists; but he remains the man that he was when he was unknown and poor in his solitude at Brussels.

He likes few things, but likes those thoroughly. He reads little, but what he reads strikes home to him as to no one else; Baudelaire and Rousseau, in whom he delights, are instances. He is passionately fond of music, especially of Gluck, but seldom speaks of it. He simplifies everything, sees only the main lines in morality as in art, lives by two or three principles, and has an aversion for everything that is not essential.

When one knows Rodin well one ceases to be able to separate him from his work. He can no longer think otherwise than symbolically by slow deposits of accumulated sensation which work on in the deep strata of his consciousness and suddenly blossom and take a name. His statues are states of the soul. He is himself a representative being, surprised at his own immanence, and his intelligence is outdone by his instinct. That is how it comes about that he does not always know how to name the beings that he has discovered, as we discover, by means of pain, corners of our consciousness that we had not suspected. In the same way that Rodin seems to break away the fragments of a block from around an already existing statue hidden in it, he is himself a sort of rock concealing shapes within it and embracing in its secret recesses immense crystallised arborescences. With a simple enough personal psychology he expresses infinite shades and inflexions of emotion. His thought is like the monad of Leibnitz; it seems, when one sees the man, to have no window to the outer world.

Rodin's opinions upon social life are vague. He contents himself with repeating that work lovingly done is the secret of all order and all happiness. To love life and natural forms, and to attempt nothing disobedient to Nature or her aims, that is his whole morality.

He sees very few people and visits nobody. He would baffle visitors accustomed to elegant, literary, well-informed, brilliant artists. His studio in the Rue de l'Université, at the end of an old yard encumbered by blocks of marble and shaded by aged chestnut trees, is like the work-place of a poor beginner. Neither a carpet nor an ornament is to be seen; the stone floor, the bare walls, a few rush chairs, some modelling stands, some cloths, a shabby deal table loaded with papers, sketches piled up on shelves, blouses hanging on nails, a cast-iron stove – these and nothing more are found by the many foreign admirers who come to see Rodin, and whom he receives with invariable amiability amid his assistants at work upon the Hugo monument or upon some smaller piece of marble.

Setting aside his journeys to London and Prague and his travels in Germany and Italy, Rodin leads an extremely retired life in Paris, and is rarely to be met. He invariably lunches at his own house at Meudon, then goes to the Rue de L'Université to work, and goes home again to dinner. Formerly, before he had his house at Meudon, he used to lunch at a *café* in the Place de L'Alma, where he was to be seen for twenty years, and to which people used to go to see him, rather as people go to see Ibsen in Christiania. The house, of a sixteenth-century style, that Rodin has inhabited at Meudon since 1900, is situated amid vineyards, and stands alone at the end of a sort of cliff, overlooking all Paris, the Seine, and the Bois de Boulogne, and facing the wooded heights of Saint Cloud and Bellevue. The site is open and fine; Rodin enjoys immense expanses of sky, sunsets, storms, and moonlight nights that delight him. The house is spacious, light, furnished with extreme simplicity, and adorned by a few pictures, the works of friends (in particular his portraits by Sargent and Legros). Rodin has added to it the pavilion in iron and glass, in which he exhibited all his work, at the Rond-point de l'Alma, in the exhibition of 1900. This pavilion, rebuilt and full of brilliant sunlight, contains all the artist's statuary. There are also several small studios, in which Rodin has his marble rough-hewn, keeps the casts of his statues or accumulates the collections of bronzes, marbles, antique or Gothic, and fragments which he is never tired of finding out and buying. In this place, which, after a life of difficulties and worries, Rodin has been able to purchase, he leads a life that fully suits his tastes, among beautiful trees and flowers, with a majestic landscape before him. It is touching to see the man, here, amid the enormous mass of his work, a whole world of statues, with which he lives and which sums up all his labours and all his existence. A photograph which I am able to add to the illustrations of this volume will give a partial idea of that surprising and imposing cohort of figures in clay, marble, and bronze – that impassioned or tragic throng. Rodin receives very few visitors at Meudon – hardly any but old friends, and he spends his mornings in his garden or in his light and cheerful studio drawing or superintending his workmen. It is chiefly at Meudon that he prepares his rough drafts, the main lines of his compositions; and in order to see an effect he will often hastily put together with clay some of the plaster limbs that he keeps in a number of glass cases – quite an anatomical museum in fact, filling a whole storey, and containing hundreds of pieces and of attitudes piled together.

Rodin appears to stand alone in his own time; first, by his genius; and secondly, by the special character of his artistic conception. This solitude, however, is only apparent. Rodin's ideas, as opposed to the teaching of the "École," form a body of logical principles which are slowly attracting the adhesion of young artists. The long struggle of impressionism against academism has now entered upon its last phase: the return to the French tradition, to national affiliation in opposition to the Roman neo-classicism. That idea, which is the programme of all independent and interesting critical intelligence in our country, finds in Rodin its perfect demonstration, and the only one afforded by contemporary sculpture. Until now Rodin has preached only by example, and we know how slow the critics and the public are in extracting from a work the ideas that it contains. But the extraction is now begun, and Rodin himself speaks with undisputed authority. Since the exhibition of 1900 his moral position stands ten times higher. Youth greets him as a chieftain and his detractors are silent. While the synthetic and symbolic mind of Rodin arouses the enthusiasm and inspires the thoughts of writers, the theory of the amplification of the modelling is making its way in the studios of sculptors. "Rodin has opened a large window in the pale house of contemporary sculpture," declares Pierre Roche, the sculptor; "out of the timid and much impaired craft that was before his day he has shown that a bold art full of hope can be made." This opinion of one of the most delicate artists of our generation is precisely that of many independent sculptors. Among these we must quote Emile Bourdelle, Rodin's pupil and friend, an impassioned, vibrating, and generous artist, whose works are among those first looked for in each Salon. Others are the two brothers Gaston and Lucien Schnegg, the latter of whom exhibited in the Salon of 1904 so beautiful a head of Aphrodite, almost worthy in the mysterious and vaporous beauty of its planes, of the ancients, and of Rodin; Jules Desbois, of the first rank in technical skill and of a violently original temperament; Alexandre Charpentier, a former collaborator of Rodin's, whose success in applied art has not turned him aside from his expressive and vigorous work in statuary; Mlle. Camille Claudel, Rodin's pupil, who is the first woman sculptor of existing-art in France, and whose name has appeared upon admirable works; and finally, Pierre Roche, although his supple and decorative fancy denies itself the expression of the tragic. The Swiss sculptor Niederhausern-Rodo, George Minne, the sculptor of Ghent, who has a powerful creative genius, not understood, and the Italian sculptor Rosso, are also partisans of Rodin's art, and so is the Englishman Bartlett. In another direction it is very interesting to note the curious reciprocal influence of Auguste Rodin and Eugène Carrière, who are united by friendship and by the same aesthetic creed. Eugène Carrière, the most profound painter of the inner life existing in the French school of to-day, has great analogies with Rodin, both as a man and as an artist. He, too, reduces his art to essentials, to the main lines and the deliberate amplification of surfaces. Thus his figures, bathed in shadow, are akin to Rodin's statues, while the latter, bathed with dewy light, seem to be pictures by Carrière. The painter becomes massive and powerful, the sculptor becomes vaporous. Rodin seeks the bland, half-shadows of Correggio, and Carrière desires that his figures should have the powerful relief of bronze. The painter sacrifices colour to the sole study of values, and by his black-and-white comes back to sculpture. Very curious is this point of junction between two great artists. Rodin is beginning to explain himself with the pen; and Eugène Carrière has, for some years past, been writing – too rarely – passages upon art of which the style is admirable and the concentration of thought astonishing, passages which recall Mallarmé and Baudelaire, and leave far behind the commonplaces of journalistic criticism. Rodin and Carrière have their school, their circle of chosen admirers, and their double influence may soon be the most decisive, if not the most brilliant and the noisiest, in French art of to-day.

The prevailing note of opinion about Rodin among his friends and his detractors is that he is like no one else, and that no statue can, in a manner, be looked at beside his, so individual is the conception from which they spring. By the mere fact that they exist, they compel us to choose between them and the others. Their silhouettes, their planes, the quality of their shadows, and their lights, make them technically works apart. If such a man understands sculpture thus, either he is right, against everybody, or he is totally mistaken; we cannot like him and also approve of ordinary statuary. His psychological and tragic genius conquers the admiration even of those who oppose his material execution. Rodin does not set himself up as a chief, nor recognise followers; yet he is a chief by his very work.

He is the greatest living French artist, and one of the most complex and powerful movers of thought in modern art. He does not found a school, but he influences the soul of a generation. He remains alone, not susceptible of imitation; but if he did not exist sculpture would be deprived of its greatest regenerator.[*1] By inscribing passions in symbols, he touches the sensibilities of all, and is a master to poets as much as to sculptors, because his subjects are moral, affecting, never commanded by an anecdote, bathed in the universally lyric. Attempts have been made to blame him because of the admiration of writers; it has been said, with an inflexion of scorn (especially in the circles of his fellow-artists), "he is a *littéraire.*" An injustice easily committed at a time when the intellect of painters and sculptors seems to blush at itself, and when they make it a sort of false merit to show that their eye and hand are separate from their brain. Rodin's splendid technical power annuls the reproach and retains the praise. Resting firmly upon nature, his symbols may rise high. Rodin delights poets because he makes the infinite emanate from the most finite of arts.

Everything has been patiently meditated by him. He dares, but is never overbold; his balance and his taste are those of a classic, despite the uncomprehending astonishment of the academic sculptors, hypnotised by the sophistry of *finish* and *elegance*, and confusing the *exact* with the *true*. There is a synthesized form, that corresponds to reality synthesized in symbols, a *second truth;* and that proportion is observed by very few artists. Most of them, contenting themselves with an immediate, momentary, anecdotic truth, translate it by picturesque observation, or by minutely detailed copying. This attempt of a sterile cleverness to transcribe the instantaneous is the very contrary of art, the first character of which is to display the laws of vital permanence underlying fugitive aspects. Herein lies the reason why sculptors become uneasy over Rodin, while writers, more familiar with general ideas, become enthusiastic. The impressionist crisis – the study, that is to say, of instantaneous lights and actions – hardly got over, he brings in this *second truth,* the transcription of general and permanent feelings into a form that speaks as much to the mind as to the senses. Such a man dominates impressionism as much as he does academism.

A whole order of curious and fundamental relations between nervous sensibility and thought has arisen out of his work. Rodin's personality is specially representative in the line of French sculptors. He goes back, as I have said, to the Egyptians and the Greeks in the matter of technical ideas. In his tragic feeling he proceeds directly from the Gothic artists. It is from them that he descends, and especially from the sculptors of the French

Renascence, in particular Germain Pilon; and he blends his Greek remembrances, passed through an Italian influence, with a conception altogether national, vigorous, and decorative. Rodin's actual part is to take up sculpture exactly at the moment of the French evolution.[*2] Since that time we have had some great masters; native genius has been triumphantly upheld, in opposition to the false school that came from the Alps, by Coysevox, Houdon, Puget, Pajou, Pigalle, Clodion, Falconet, Couston, Rude, Carpeaux, and Barye, a line of splendid inventors of shapes, all of whom, in contradistinction to the official school, have represented the inmost qualities of their race. All these men Rodin emulates by the importance of his work; perhaps the future may regard him as the magnificent outcome of their efforts carried on through three centuries. In this succession of artists, Puget, Rude, and Barye are those with whom his technical relations are closest.[*3] But he has been less decorative than Puget and less hampered by the themes imposed upon him; he has gone further than the great Rude in the expression of inward emotion, and he surpasses even Barye in power of modelling and boldness of silhouette. He has created a world which is fully his own, a feeling and a pathos not to be found elsewhere, which are the very soul of his time.

Rodin, then, can be set only beside Puget and Rude. Like Puget, he is overflowing with vitality and with passionate frenzy; he worships power and heroic beings; but his are sad, and nearer to Gothic asceticism and to the nervous derangement of Baudelaire than to the resplendent pomp of the seventeenth century, into which Puget transposed his heroes of Rome and of Corneille. Like Rude, he is attracted by deep things, by soul tragedies; but he is more abstract than the creator of the *Napoleon Awakening to Immortality,* the *Joan of Arc,* or the *Marseillaise.* Rodin is more general, more synthetic; he turns his mind to permanent symbols, outside of ages and races. Taking up, as if in challenge, the mythological subjects that the "École" had most spoiled, he has shown how a great mind can renew all things and impress upon them the magic of its vision. He is the most symbolic of our men of genius; and if the modelling of the Greeks, Gothic austerity, the strength of Puget and of Rude, have helped Rodin to make up his personality, the fusion of these elements and the addition of a personal imagination and an extraordinary contemplative faculty have enabled him, like Wagner, who descended from Bach, Beethoven, and Liszt, to create, after and apart from all of them, work that resumes them and forgets them, to become in its turn an initiator. The point in which Rodin is inimitable is the expression of the voluptuous with all its latent woes; and this point strongly recalls to memory *Tristan and Isolde*, which is such a paroxysm as might touch the most perilous region of exceptional art; but Rodin is kept within the bounds of the normal, and protected from the audacities of his strange and troubled imagination, by his imperturbable technical certainty and by his admiration for some few masters. As was the case with Baudelaire and with Poe, his purity and grandeur of form save him; like Dante, this lover of gloomy beauty hangs over the verge of passion's hell without falling into it.

Rodin's art is healthy because it feeds upon natural truth and general logic. He is the supreme painter of man bowed by intense, melancholic, feverish, constricting thought; but also, with a candid tenderness unknown to Wagner, he is the caressing creator of women in love, the poet of youth, embracing and radiant. Only a genius can have the diversity of mind that produces *The Burghers of Calais*, ascetic and mediæval, the spasmodic *Hell*, the almost abstract *Balzac*, the bronze busts worthy of Donatello, and the images of women carved in the radiant and golden marble of Attica by a sensuous and subtle enthusiast who has rediscovered the soul of Hellenic beauty. This union of technical skill, evolved according to the secrets of the antique with a power of expressing all human sentiments from gentleness to lewdness, from the mystic to the pathetic, from nervous disorganisation to carnal frankness, this union of contraries and this universality are not to be found in any of our forerunners. Not Puget, nor Rude, nor any of our masters has had such intellectual ubiquity, such strength of condensation; in these points it is allowable, even in our own day, to acknowledge Rodin as supreme in the rich French school, and thus to anticipate the judgment of the future, in whose eyes he will loom yet larger.

In any case it was high time he should appear; he has been as useful as was Manet by his intervention in French art. In spite of Dalou, sculpture had fallen very low after the death of Carpeaux and Barye; the deplorable school of the Second Empire had brought it into degeneracy, and we could reckon no one in sculpture to correspond to the great impressionists. Such men as Dujalbert, Chapu, Mercié, Frémiet, Saint Marceaux, and Falguière, are but sham great sculptors, nothing of whose work will last; the "École" group, from Paul Dubois to Barrias, Aube and Guillaume, is a mere example of pretentious insignificance. The few vigorous temperaments, or workers of genuine technical merit, like Denys Puech, Jean Dampt, Gardet, Camille Lefèvre, Devillez, and Jean Bassier, did not know how to put together their efforts in such a way as to found a real school. They produced without attaining a cohesion of thought capable of guiding a fresh generation. Bartholomé, thoughtful, pure, dreamy, and proud, stands apart. Mme. Besnard and M. Théodore Rivière are charming, but without influence. I have spoken of the group that has spontaneously placed itself around Rodin. Amid this interesting, unequal, and scattered sculpture he appeared with the authority of a master and a prophet; his work set the question upon its true basis again, showing whence we came, what was to be avoided, and whither we were to go; and all this with such clearness of evidence that the appearance of Rodin becomes, in like degree with that of Goujon and that of Puget, a capital date in the history of the French school, I declared in the Preface my intention to avoid any extravagant eulogy of Rodin, and have uttered my dislike of the idolatry by which some people think it necessary publicly to emphasise their admiration, with its snobbish accretions. But I should fall into the opposite fault if I did not declare the truth and the importance of what such an artist brings to his art, and did not mark his exact place in the line of his country's sculpture. Henley has called Rodin the Michelangelo of the modern world. That opinion of a foreign critic, a critic justly esteemed one of the most upright in contemporary literature, France may justly make her own, far from extravagant and puerile praises, and in the face of the work accomplished. I shall be but too happy if I have contributed to make clearer to the public certain secret reasons, certain inner frameworks, of that logical and beautiful work.

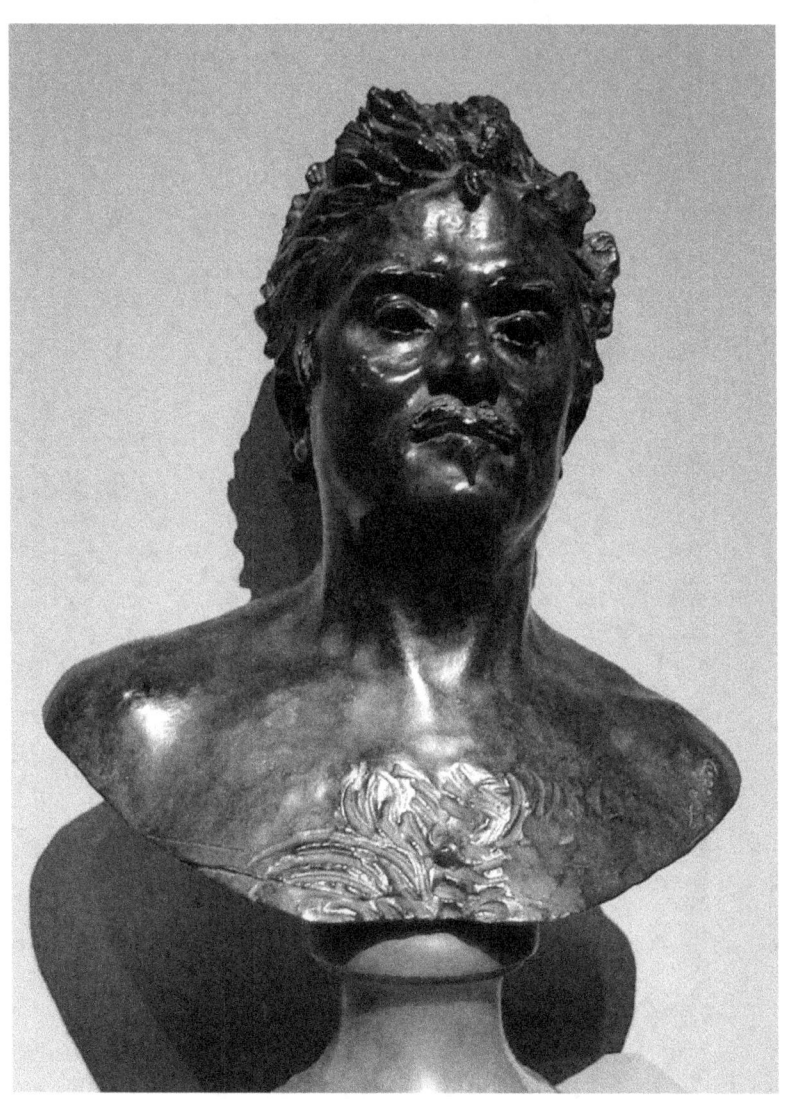

Auguste Rodin, Bust of Balzac, 1892

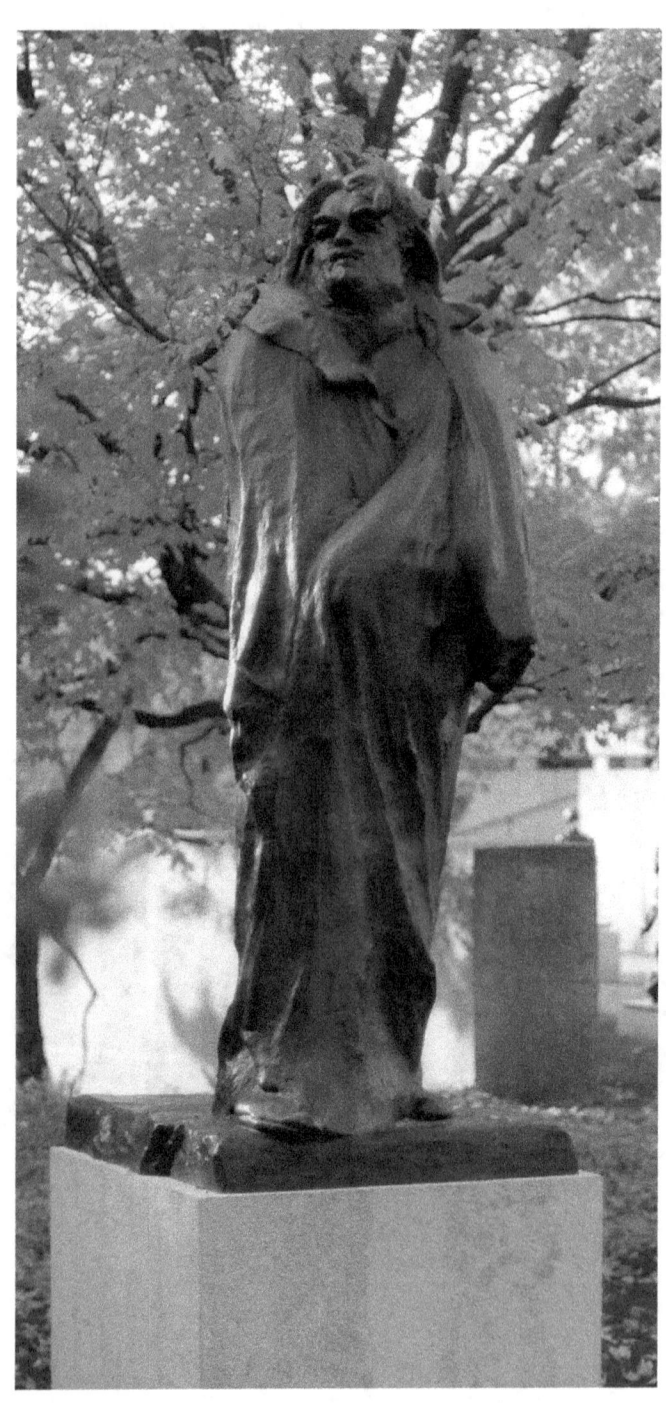

Auguste Rodin, Monument To Balzac

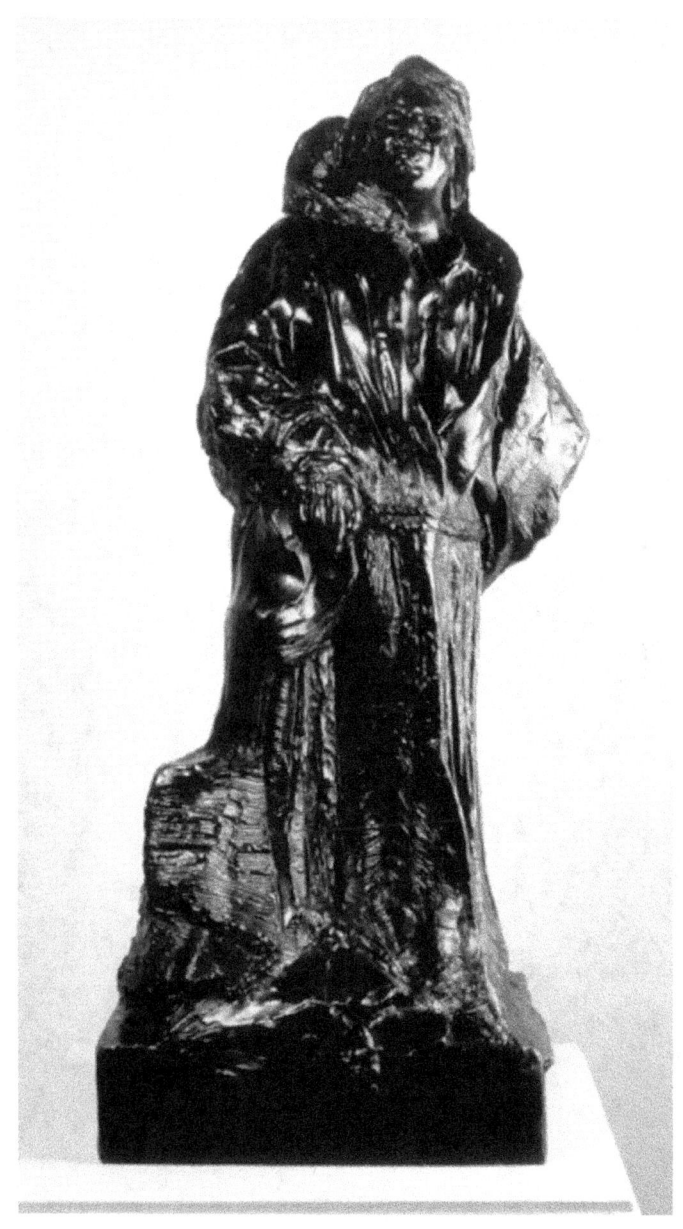

Auguste Rodin, Balzac

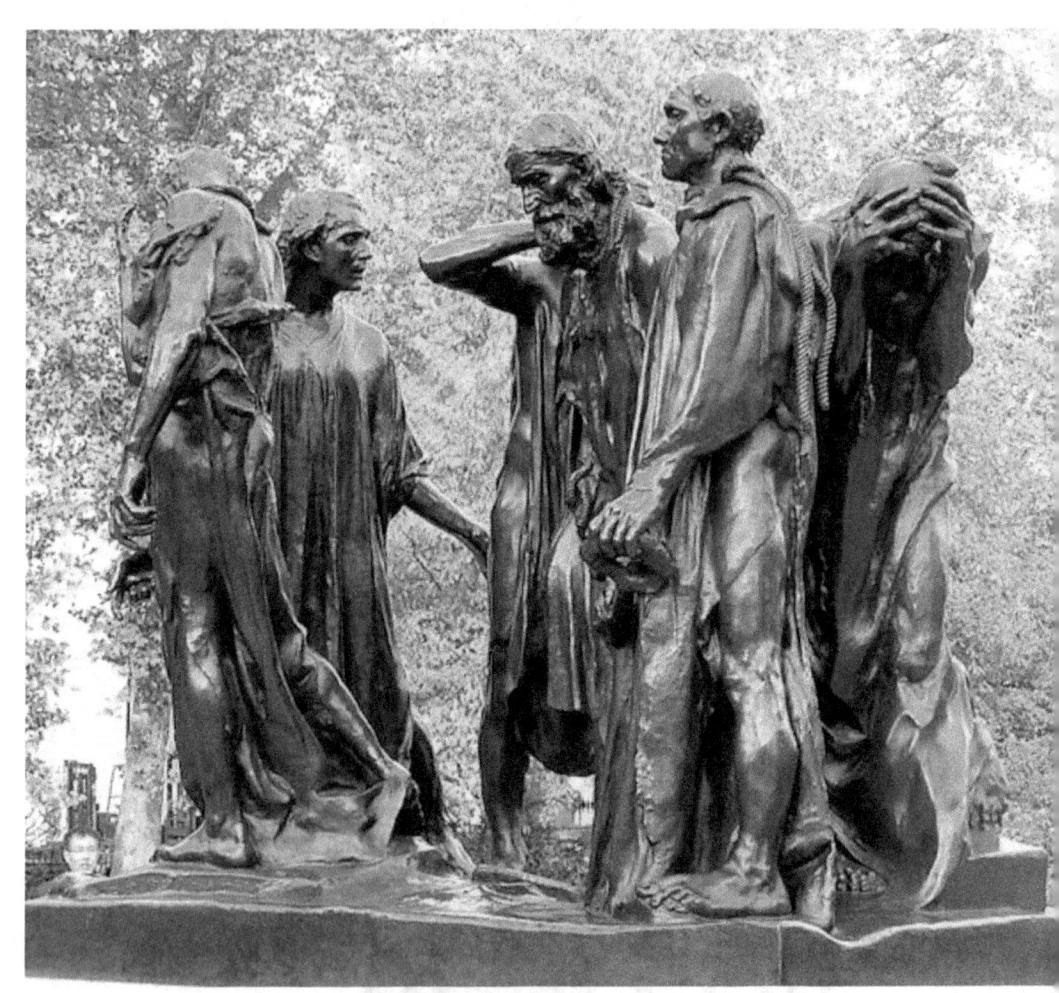

Auguste Rodin, The Burghers of Calais

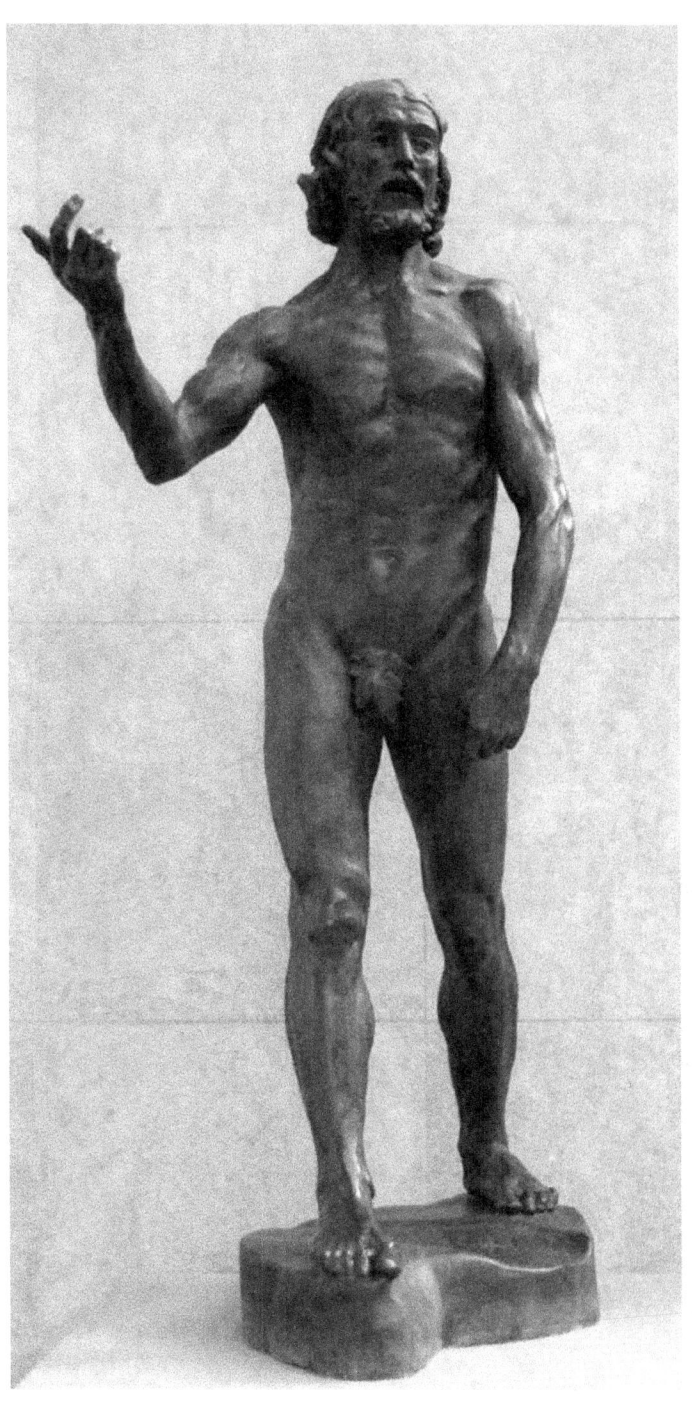

Auguste Rodin, St John the Baptist Preaching

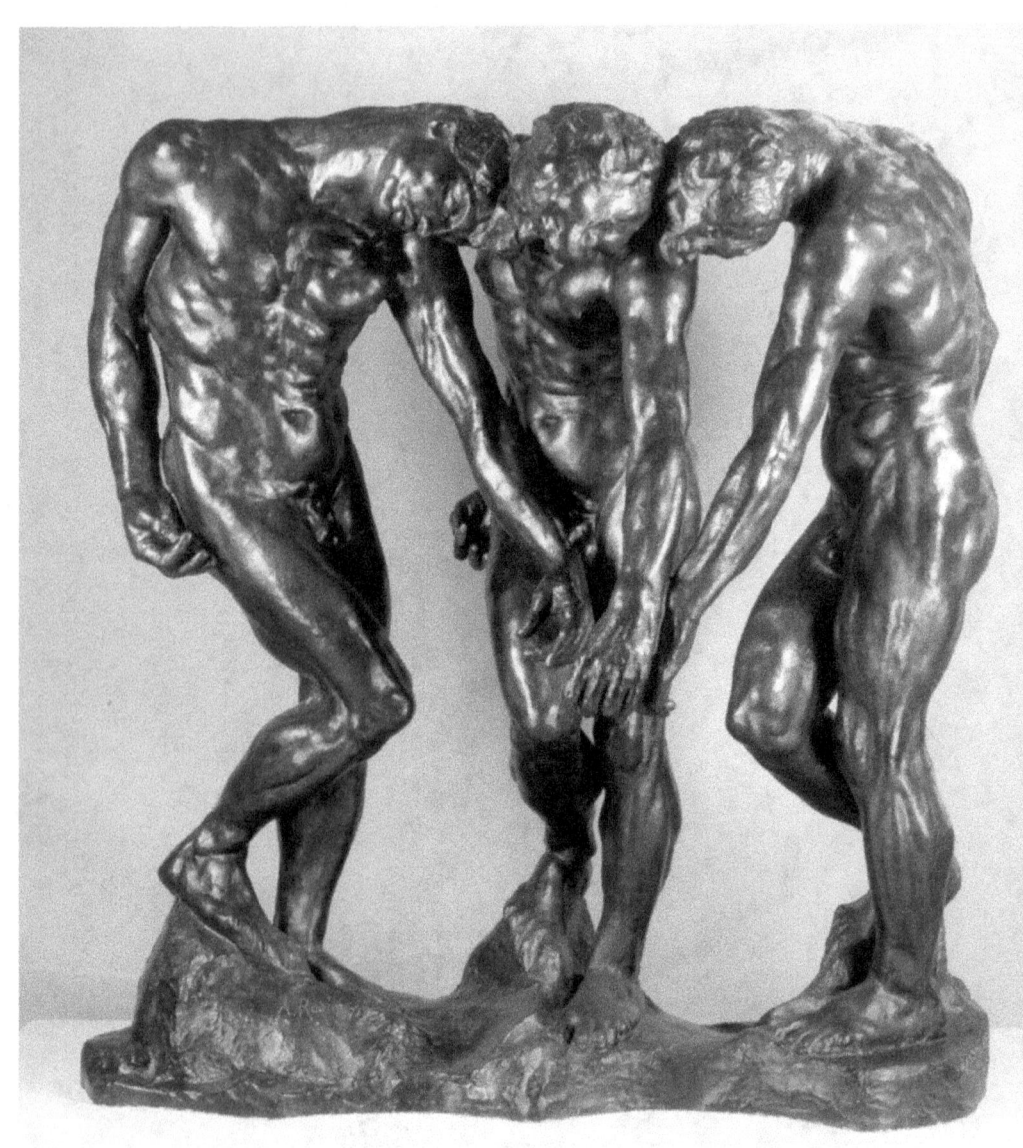

Auguste Rodin, The Three Shadows, 1880

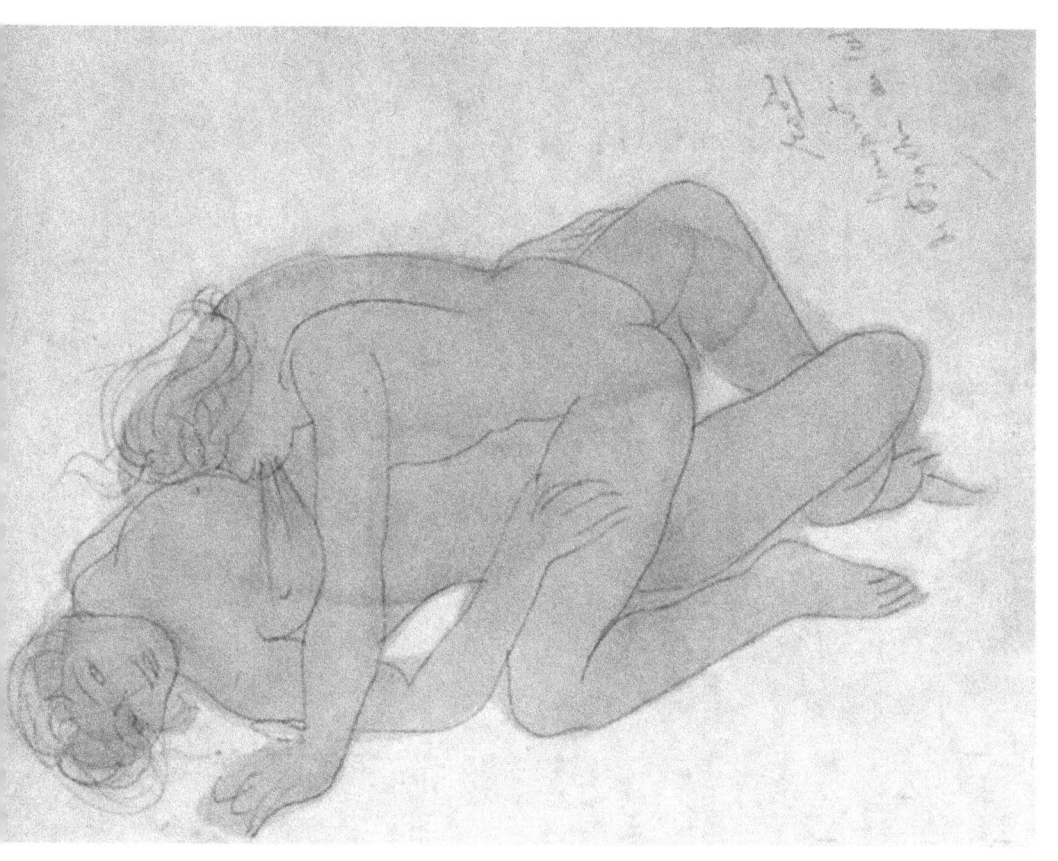

Auguste Rodin, nude drawings (this page and following)

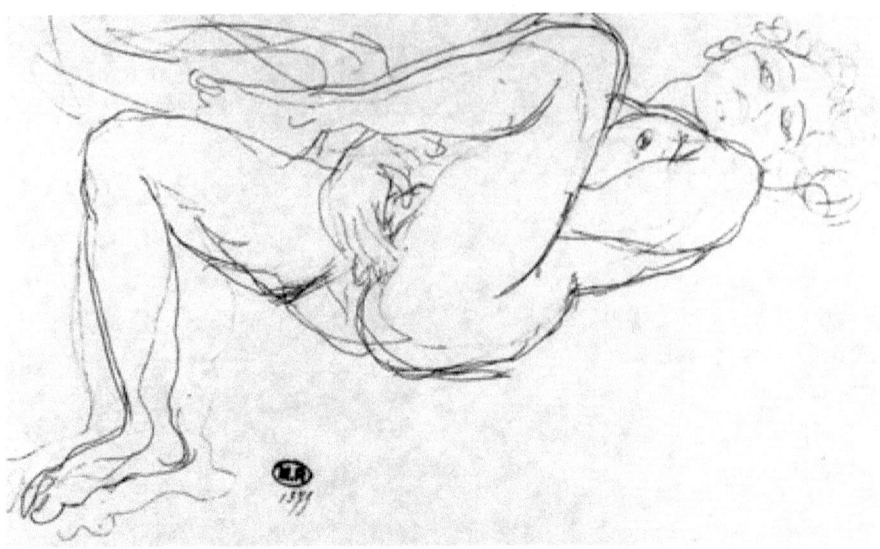

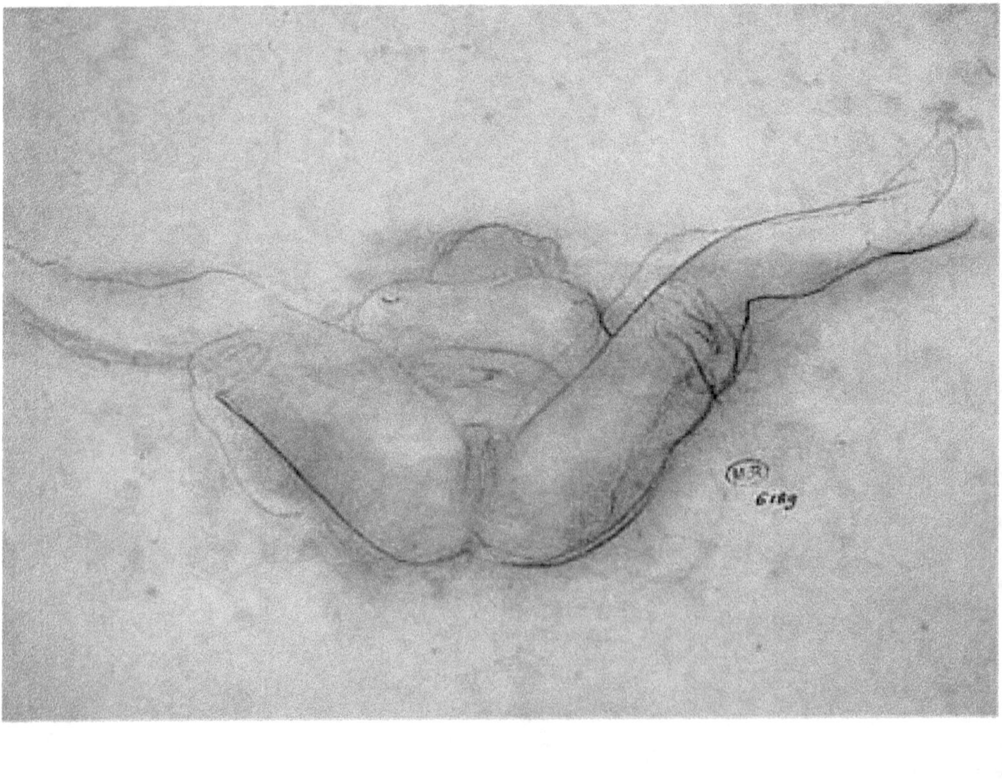

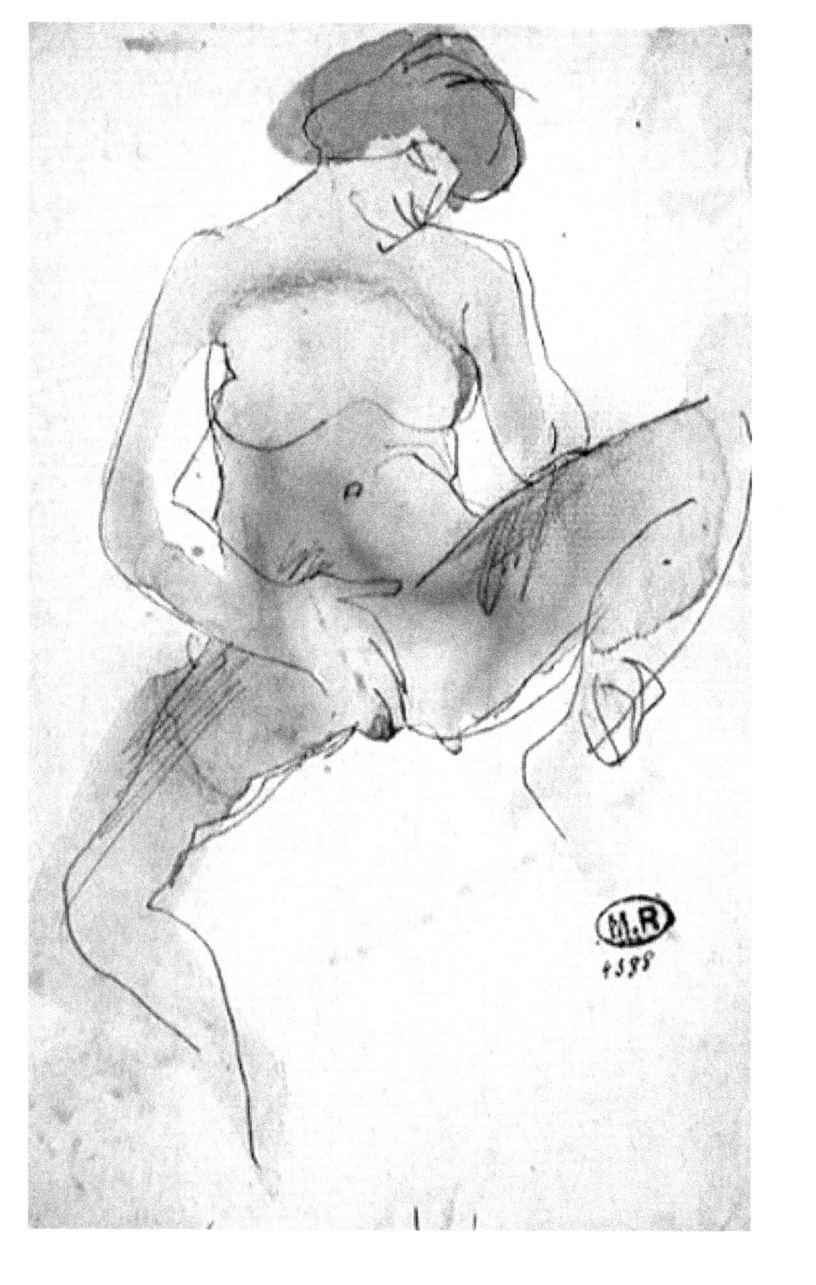

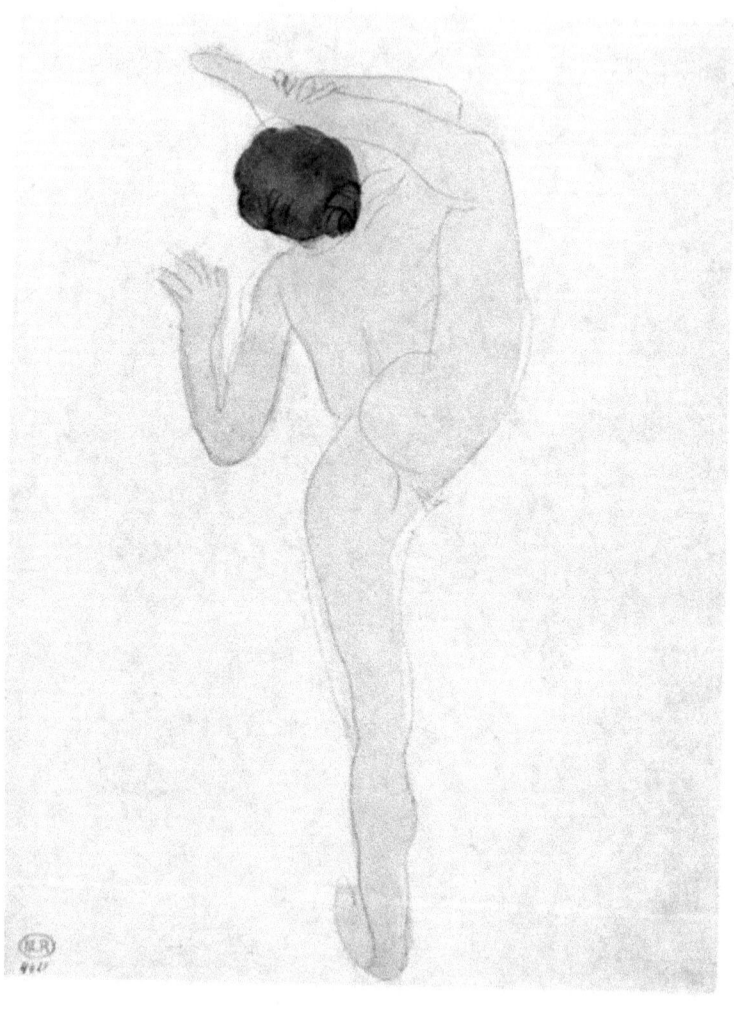

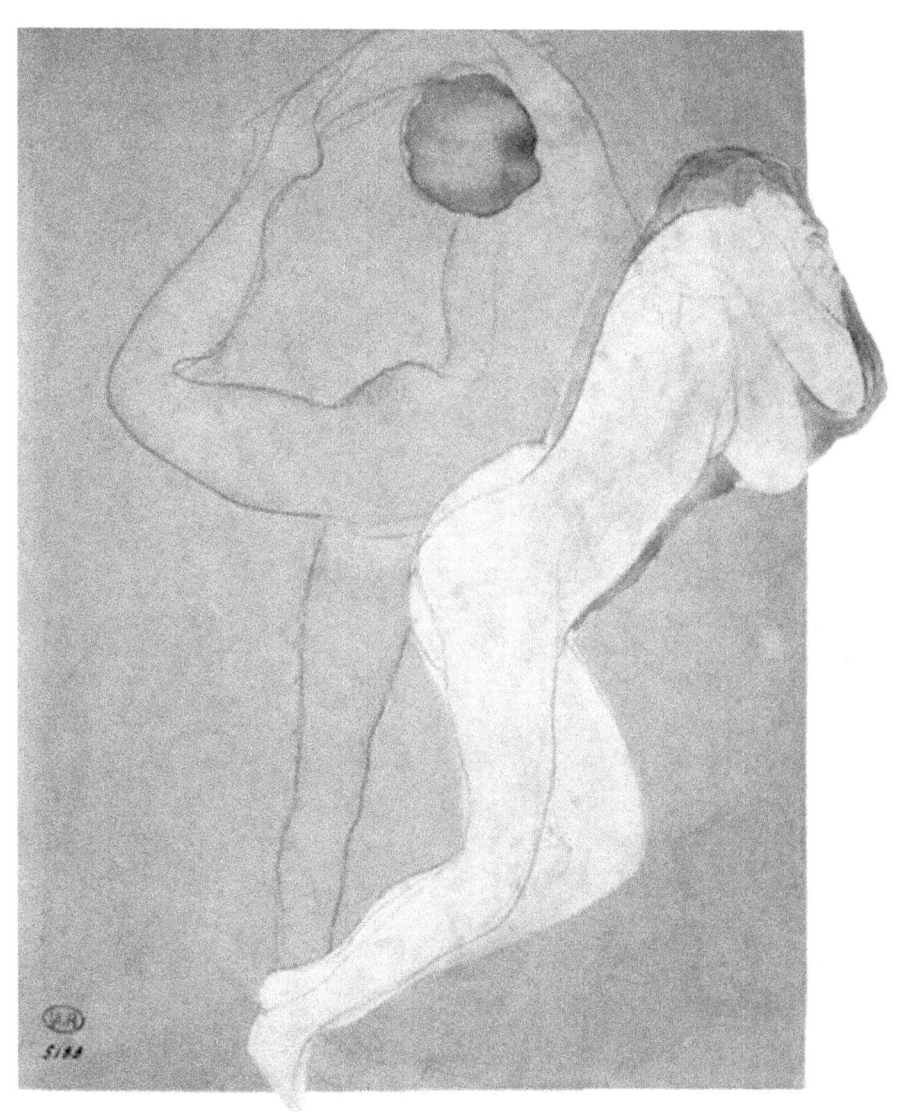

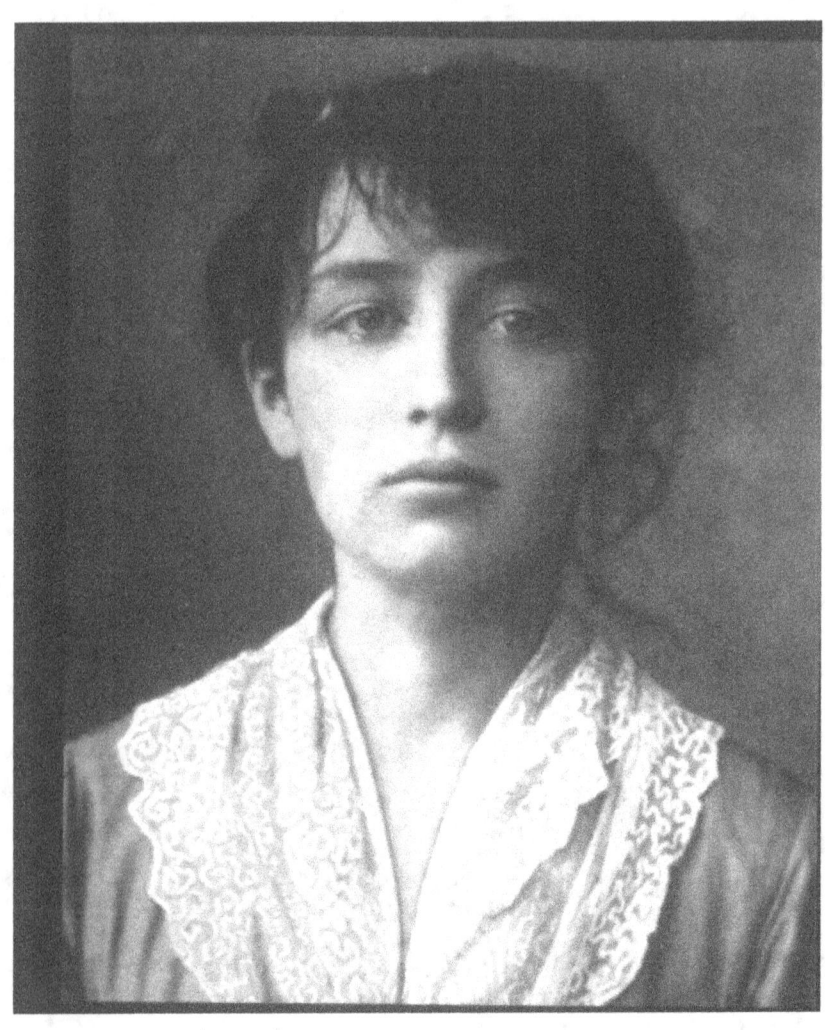

Camille Claudel, before 1883

VI

APPENDIX – CHRONOLOGICAL LIST OF RODIN'S
PRINCIPAL WORKS – LIST OF THE PRINCIPAL BOOKS OR
ARTICLES WRITTEN ABOUT HIM – QUOTATIONS
REFERRING TO HIM – AN OPINION OF EUGÈNE
CARRIÈRE'S; AN OPINION OF HENLEY'S – VARIOUS NOTES

Chronological catalogue of Rodin's works is almost impossible to
draw up. I do not think Rodin himself could do it. It must be
remembered that before 1877 he made a quantity of studies which
he destroyed, and such a producer as he is willing to neglect
things of which others would keep count. In his poor and
wandering days Rodin must have abandoned many things. How
would it be possible to recount the figures that were retouched or
even executed at Carrier-Belleuse's, the earliest independent
works, the characters executed by him at Brussels, the statues that
were planned and left unfinished for lack of money, those that
were broken or that failed – all the immense store of work
accomplished in the course of twenty years by a man who worked
every day? How would it be possible even to enumerate the
sketches and varied renderings of different subjects piled up in
the studio at Meudon, in the Clos Payen, in the Rue des
Fourneaux, and at Vaugirard? It is a whole world. I will confine
myself, therefore, to a statement of known and exhibited works:
and these, indeed, are what is essential.

LIST OF THE PRINCIPAL
EXHIBITED WORKS

1864. *The Man with a Broken Nose.*

1865-70. Works in the studio of Carrier-Belleuse.

1872-77. Friezes upon the Bourse and various works at Brussels.

1877. *The Primitive Man (The Age of Brass).* Decorative work on the Trocadéro.

1878-80. *Saint Jerome. Saint John the Baptist.* Works in the manufactory of Sèvres. Competition for the National Defence Monument.

1881. *Adam* (destroyed). *Eve.*

1882. *Ugolino* (a sketch taken up again later). Busts of *Alphonse Legros* and *IV. E. Henley.* Studies for *The Gate of Hell.*

1883. *Bellona. General Lynch* (equestrian statue). *The Genius of War.*

1884. *Monument of President Vicunha. Bust of a Young Woman.*

1885. *The Man and the Serpent.* Busts of *Dalou, Hugo,* and *Antonin Proust.*

1886. First sketch of the Hugo monument. Drawings dealing with *The Gate of Hell.* Bust of *Henry Becque. The Kiss* (a small group).

1887. *Perseus and the Gorgon. Head of St. John beheaded.*

1888. *The Danaid. Alan Walking.* Nude study for one of the

Burghers of Calais. Several little groups.

1889. Studies for the *Gate of Hell* and the monument to *Claude Lorraine. Torso of a Woman.* Group of *The Dream. The Dream of Life. Women Damned* (in marble). *Hecuba.* Bust of *Roger Marx. Destitution. Thought* (in marble).

1890. *Bust of a Young Woman* (in silver). *Torso of Saint John. Brother and Sister.*

1891. *The Caryatid. The Young Mother. A Nymph.*

1892. Busts of *Puvis de Chavannes* and *Henri Rochefort. Grief. Claude Lorraine. The Burghers of Calais.*

1893. *The Death of Adonis.* Medallion of *César Franck. Galatea.* Bust of *Séverine. The Crest and the Wave. Resurrection. The Child Achilles* (group in clay).

1894. *Eternal Spring. Hope* (a reclining figure in back view.) *Orpheus and Eurydice* (first version). *Christ and Magdalen.*

1895. Inauguration of *The Burghers of Calais. Illusion, the Daughter of Icarus.* Medallion of *Octave Mirbeau.* Nude studies for the *Balzac. Man Crouching.*

1896. *The Inner Voice. The Muse of Anger* (for the Hugo monument). *The Conqueror. Minerva. The Poet and the Life of Contemplation. Women Bathing.* Studies for the *Balzac.*

1897. *Victor Hugo. Balzac.* Monument of *President Sarmiento.*

1898. Statue of *Balzac.* Bust of a *Young American.* Bust of *Madame F.* Statue of *Sarmiento,* with a high relief of Apollo in marble. Monument of *Labour. The Benedictions* (marble). *Twilight. Clouds. The Parcæ and the Young Girl.*

1899. Works for the Hugo monument.

1900. Marble groups. Exhibition at the Rond-point de l'Alma.

1901. *Shades* (for *The Gate of Hell*).

1902. Groups in marble. *The Hand of God.* Busts.

1903. Bust of *Hugo. The Poet and the Muse.* Various sketches. *Ugolino* (fresh version). *The Prodigal Son.*

1904. *The Thinker,* and various works in marble in process of execution.[*1]

The work of Rodin may thus be estimated at about ten works

on a grand scale, forty groups or statues, some thirty important busts, and perhaps two hundred figures or portraits, without counting sketches, from 1877 to 1904.

I come now to the mention of some significant writings that deal with his aesthetic theory or with his work; and, as may be supposed, I leave out of question a quantity of valueless articles, for Rodin has been directly or indirectly the pretext for a great mass of writings, and is the modern French artist who has been most talked of, justly or unjustly. The works quoted are such as may be consulted with advantage.

ARTICLES OR BOOKS
RELATING TO RODIN

"Balzac and Rodin," by *Roger Marx (Le Voltaire,* March, 1892).

"Claude Lorraine," by Roger Marx *(Le Voltaire,* June, 1892). (Excellent studies in the criticism of sculpture.)

"Auguste Rodin," by Roger Marx *(Pan,* a n d *The Image,* September, 1897).

Drawings by Rodin, 129 plates, containing 142 heliogravures (Goupil and Co., 1897), from the suggestions and loans of M. Fenaille.

"Rodin's Studio," by Edouard Rod *(Gazette des Beaux Arts,* May, 1898).

"Rodin," by Gabriel Mourey *(Revue illustrée,* October, 1899)

Exhibition of 1900: Rodin's Works, with four prefaces by Eugène Carrière, Jean Paul Laurens, Claude Monet, and Albert Besnard.

"Rodin and Legros," by Arsène Alexandre *(Figaro,* June, 1900).

"The Gate of Hell," by Anatole France *(Figaro,* June 1st, 1900).

La Revue des Beaux Arts et des Lettres, January 1st, 1900.

La Plume, 1900. Special number.

Les Maîtres Artistes, special number, October 15th, 1903. (Illustrated collections, containing a certain number of critical studies by various authors.)

Rodin, by Léon Riotor: a pamphlet, reproducing in French,

German, English, Italian, Spanish, and Russian, a study that appeared in the *Revue populaire des Beaux Arts,* April 8th, 1899.

Rodin, the Sculptor, a volume of criticism, illustrated; by Léon Maillard (Floury); 1899.

The Sculptor Rodin, drawn from life. A volume by Mlle. Judith Cladel (*La Plume* office, 1903).

Rodin, a study by L. Brieger-Wasser (Vogel. Strassburg; 1903).

Rodin, by George Treu (*Jahrbuch der bildenden Kunst.* Berlin, Marstersteig, 1903).

Rodin, by R. M. Rilke (Berlin, Bard, 1903).

"Rodin." Articles upon, by W. E. Henley, 1890; D. S. MacColl, 1902; Henri Duhem, 1890; Karel B. Made (Prague); Vittorio Pica (Rome).

Of these various writings devoted to Rodin, those of Roger Marx should be particularly noted, on account of their technical understanding; Léon Maillard's volume is a sincere, well-informed, well-illustrated book, produced by a man who comprehends. The book by Mlle. Judith Cladel, daughter of the distinguished novelist, is an originally conceived volume, the only one that relates certain conversations, and attempts, with charming acuteness, to present Rodin in his private character. It is a work that deserves to be much better known and appreciated, and of which Rodin's first panegyrists, jealous of being the only "inventors" of the artist, have been very careful not to speak. The article by the graceful painter, Henri Duhem, is likewise excellent; and I consider Mr. MacColl's very remarkable, on account of its elevation and precision of judgment. The others have such value as belongs to admiring articles written hurriedly in newspapers: they express sympathetic feelings, or comment in a poetical way upon the subjects, but their critical value is négligeable, and there is nothing to be quoted from them for the information of my readers. The *Balzac* gave rise to a shoal of newspaper articles. Georges, Rodenbach, and France, on that occasion, said the acute and witty thing's about Rodin that they say about all manifestations of thought, and M. Mirbeau made Rodin the theme of some of those polemical variations, conjoining hyperbolical praise with abuse of his adversaries, which he is accustomed to offer as art-criticisms, and which have gained him a reputation of a certain kind. There is nothing to note in these pamphlets mixed with eulogistic effusions, the whole of which do not contain the substance of twenty lines by Henley or of Eugène Carrière's admirable Preface, which I am desirous of reproducing here because it is a masterpiece of synthetic divination.[*2]

THE ART OF RODIN

"Rodin's art comes from the earth and returns to it, like those giant blocks – rocks or dolmens – which mark deserts, and in the heroic grandeur of which man recognises himself.

"The transmission of thought by art, like the transmission of life, is the work of passion and of love.

"Passion, whose obedient servant Rodin is, makes him discover the laws that serve to express it; she it is that gives him the sense of volumes and proportions, the choice of the expressive prominence.

"Thus the earth projects external apparent forms, images, and statues that fill us with a sense of its internal life.

"These terrestrial forms were the real guides of Rodin. They have set him free from scholastic traditions, in them he found his being and the creative instinct of men whom humanity celebrates.

"Trees and plants revealed to him their likeness to those fair women, with sleek limbs rising, like delicate columns, to the moving torso and swelling breast, above which the head hangs heavily in the company of a strong and supple neck, even as a fine fruit full of savour weighs down its branch.

"The massive brow overshadows the eyes, and the cheek brings the lip softly to the lover's entreaty.

"Forms seek and meet in voluptuous desires of violence and of resignation, rebellious and obedient to laws from which nothing escapes; everywhere conscious logic triumphs.

"The generalising spirit of Rodin has imposed solitude upon him. It has not been his lot to work upon the cathedral that is not, but his desire of humanity links him to the eternal forms of nature."

After such a passage, in which every word is significant and eloquent, and is a great artist's reflection, everything seems pale. I will not, however, confine myself to a mere dry mention of the essay by Vittorio Pica, the great Italian critic, who generously arranged for Rodin's participation in the Venetian Exhibition (Gallery of Modern Art, 1897), and I should have liked to quote Anatole France's fine article, and some assertions of Mr. MacColl's, who very logically recalls to our memory the sculptor Auguste Préault, who is too much forgotten, and who was, indeed, a sort of imperfect precursor of Rodin. I must at least transcribe a few lines from W. E. Henley, who was, from the very beginning, a clear-sighted admirer of Rodin, and who spoke of him with eloquence and passion: –

"M. Dalou ... has declared that when the century goes out it will remember the aforesaid doors" (i.e. *The Gate of Hell*) "as its heroic achievement in sculpture. And if that be true – as I believe it to be true – then where, between himself and Michelangelo, is there so lofty a head as Rodin's?... His busts alone were enough to place him in the future, the style of them is so complete, the treatment so large and so distinguished, the effect so personal, yet so absolute in art.... Here, if you will, are a thousand hints of the possibilities of human passion: from Paolo and Francesca melting into each other:

"'La bocca mi bacio tutta tremante'

as no man and woman have done in sculpture since sculpture began.... Here is sculpture in its essence.... You may read into it as much literature as you please, or as you can; but the interpolation is not Rodin's, but your own.... It is not literature in relief, nor literature in the round; it is sculpture pure and simple.... Passion is with him wholly a matter of form and surface and line, and exists not apart from these.... He is our Michelangelo; and if he had not been that, he might have been our Donatello. And with Phidias and Lysippus all these some-and-twenty centuries afar, what more is left to say of the man of genius whose art is theirs?"

We see that Henley's admiration returns to the comparison of Michelangelo and Rodin. I persist in thinking that the resemblance rather lies in moral identity, in conception than in technicalities. The muscular enlargement of the Italian hero is not Rodin's amplification nor his expressiveness, *which is altogether nervous*. It is none the less true that these two men are the only ones who have imagined and realised a sculpturesque conception of so vast a reach. Not even Puget and Rude, who came between them, ventured such wholes as *The Tomb of the Medici* or *The Gate of Hell*.

MUSEUMS

Rodin has in the Luxembourg Museum (Paris) the following works: –

The Age of Brass, originally placed in the Luxembourg Gardens near the School of Mines.

The Danaid (marble).

Thought (marble).

St. John the Baptist Preaching (bronze).

The Fair Helmet-maker (bronze).

Bust of *Jean Paul Laurens* (bronze).

The Kiss (marble).

Bust of *Mme. V.* (marble).

At the Petit Palais (Ville de Paris), one work.

At Beziers, Cognac, Dijon, Douai, Lille, and Lyons, several works.

At Brussels, one work.

At Copenhagen, several works.

At New York, Boston, Chicago, and Philadelphia, works. At Helsingfors, one work.

At Rotterdam, one work.

At Geneva (Rath Museum), three works.

At Venice, Christiania, St. Petersburg, Stockholm, Düsseldorf, Munich, Weimar, Vienna, Prague (town hall), one work in each town.

At Hamburg, three works.

At Hagen, three works.

At Berlin (new gallery of Charlottenburg), five works.

At Crefeld, two works.

At Buda-Pest, five works.

In London (Victoria and Albert Museum), two works; (British Museum), one work.

At Glasgow, one work.

Museum of Marseilles, *The Inner Voice* (clay).

The new works in these various museums are originals or casts.

PRIVATE COLLECTIONS

M. Vever (*Eve,* in marble).

M. Pontremoli (the *National Defence.*)

M. Antony Roux (*The Kiss*).

M. Roger Marx (bust, *The Young Mother*).

M. Blanc (*The Eternal Idol.*)

M. Desmarais (the *Idyll.*)

Mme. Durand (*Thought,* in marble, given to the Luxembourg).

M. Peytel (various groups).

Mme. Russell (*Minerva.*)

M. Fenaille (*The Spring, Bust of Mme. F., The Poet and the Life of Contemplation,* a twisted column with figures, surmounted by a mask).

Baron Vitta (high-reliefs in stone).

The Marquise de Carcano (*Head of St. John beheaded,* marble).

This, of course, is a very cursory list, and includes only collections in Paris.

I must add separately to the works published about Rodin those for which I am responsible: (1) a study, called "The Art of M. Rodin," *Revue des Revues,* 15th June, 1898; this has been approved by the artist, and very frequently reproduced. (2) A lecture delivered on the 31st of July, 1900, at the Rodin exhibition, and published by *La Plume,* with four unpublished drawings. (3)

An essay upon the surroundings, personality, and influence of Rodin, which appeared in the *Revue Universelle* in 1901, and has likewise been reprinted, particularly in the *Maîtres Artistes* (special number, 15th October, 1903).

The high price of the work published by Messrs. Goupil (*A Hundred and Forty-two Drawings by Rodin*) prevents that fine volume from being accessible to the public. The amateur photographer Druet has taken photographs of all Rodin's work, which are rather misty, but which render admirably the caressing touch of light on the main planes, and which in a measure reproduce the artistic atmosphere of the statues. Messrs. Haweis and Coles have likewise taken some beautiful and curious proofs. More classic, but also more definite, are the fine photographs which the art publisher Buloz has recently taken, and which have been employed to illustrate this volume.

PORTRAITS

There is a remarkable portrait of Rodin by Mr. John Sargent (dating from about twenty years ago). Another, by M. Alphonse Legros (a profile), is more of a fancy head, and wears a sort of tiara. A more recent portrait has been produced by Mr. Alexander. There is a very forcible bust by Mile. Camille Claudel, as well as a bust by J. Desbois, a lithograph by Eugène Carrière, and some amusing studio sketches by Mile. Cladel. An interesting lithograph of "Rodin in his Studio," by W. Rothenstein, appeared in the *Artist-Engraver*, April, 1904.

A curious photograph, taken by M. Steichen; a poster for the Rodin exhibition, containing a portrait, and drawn by Carrière; and some excellent photographs taken at Prague (of which the one here reproduced is astonishingly faithful) complete this list of likenesses.

NOTES

PREFACE

1. "The Art of Rodin," *Revue des Revues*, Paris, 15th June, 1898; and lecture, 31st July, 1900.

CHAPTER I

1. This unknown student was called Constant Simon. Rodin remembers him as a remarkable man.

2. The hanging committee of the Salon is called a "jury." — TRANS.

CHAPTER II

1. It is curious to recollect that the very fine equestrian statue of General Lynch and the monument to President Vicunha, sent to America by Rodin, were never paid for, and that, owing to revolutions, they actually disappeared, so that these works may be considered lost. Only the spoiled rough models and some photographs remain.

2. These *Shades* are a symbolic representation of men who are just dead, and who are bending down with folded hands in misery and terror gazing at the hellish crowd into which they are about to fall.

3. The final version of this group has been treated by Rodin separately, and is known by the name of *The Kiss*. The marble group is in the Museum of the Luxembourg.

4. A statue of Eustace de St. Pierre had been asked for. Rodin sent the six effigies of burghers, and this gave rise to fresh difficulties with the authorities.

CHAPTER III

1. Rodin has never forgotten Falguière's loyalty at the time of *The Age of Brass* affair.

2. A recent example in Paris is the double statue of the chemists who invented quinine. When will people understand that a discovery of this kind, however honourable, is nevertheless quite incapable of being associated with any plastic idea? The same thing is true of the statues of Chappe and Lavoisier, flanked by instruments of telegraphy and chemistry. These are ridiculous signboards, melancholy compliments translated by a tradesman's art that renders our streets hideous.

3. *Revue des Revues* (of Paris), June 15th, 1898.

4. I find myself underlining-: it is not Rodin whose voice makes this emphasis. But I am attempting to mark out in this way the formulas which spring up in his conversation, and which, collected together, will give the public an idea of his instinctive synthesis, deduced from life.

5. The word *exalté* has in this use no precise equivalent in English. "Enthusiast," as the eighteenth century knew the word — that is, with the infusion of a touch of lunacy — conies perhaps nearest. — TRANS.

6. An observation noted by Mlle. Judith Cladel in her curious volume, *Rodin, drawn from life*. (Éditions de La Plume, 1903.)

7. Loïe Fuller has obtained, by means of stuffs not wetted, the effects that the 'École' loves, because her plastic dance is logically derived from nature.

CHAPTER IV

1. This word may mean either a certain sort of dance, or the "round" of a patrol. — TRANS.

2. Album of 142 sketches, reproduced in heliogravure by M. Manzi and published by Goupil, 1897. These sketches in wash or colour have been selected according to the advice of M. Fenaille, their owner, who lent them, from the most imaginative of Rodin's drawings in his second manner.

CHAPTER V

1. A vehement but indiscriminating critic, M. Octave Mirbeau, has seen good to write, by way of affirming that Rodin's art moved him

strongly: "A style takes rise from him." I have neither the space nor the wish to recriminate; but it would be dangerous to let such artistic heresies pass without protest. Rodin is an admirable example, but to say that a style arises from him is to say that he may become the creator of a perishable formula, and to understand nothing about his art.

2. Some surprise may be felt at my having failed to insist upon the name of Michelangelo. Everybody has hit upon the obvious comparison. It is the exceeding obviousness that leads me to distrust it. Rodin is much nearer to Puget than to Michelangelo, who is muscular strength carried to heroic proportions. Rodin, like Puget, and more than Puget, is nervous strength. Rodin appears much more akin to Michelangelo than he really is. Careful study causes us more and more to leave behind that preliminary likeness which has sufficed so many critics.

3. We might perhaps say the same in regard to the great Carpeaux, too, who carried the art of movement and expression to so high a degree, and who did the same liberal work against the "École" as Rodin was to do at a later time. But their visions, aims, and minds differ profoundly.

CHAPTER VI

1. To these may be added, in 1905, a bust of the Rt. Hon. *George Wyndham,* and *The Hand of God.*

2. Preface to the Catalogue of the Rodin exhibition in the Pavillon de l'Alma, 1900. (The work mentioned above; other prefaces by Claude Monet, A. Besnard, and J. P. Laurens.)

CRESCENT MOON PUBLISHING

web: www.crmoon.com e-mail: cresmopub@yahoo.co.uk

ARTS, PAINTING, SCULPTURE

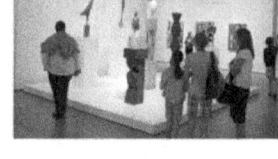
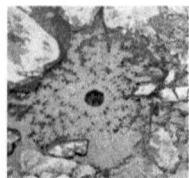
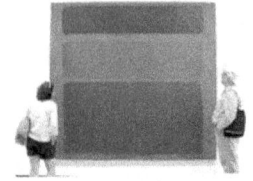

The Art of Andy Goldsworthy
Andy Goldsworthy: Touching Nature
Andy Goldsworthy in Close-Up
Andy Goldsworthy: Pocket Guide
Andy Goldsworthy In America
Land Art: A Complete Guide
The Art of Richard Long
Richard Long: Pocket Guide
Land Art In the UK
Land Art in Close-Up
Land Art In the U.S.A.
Land Art: Pocket Guide
Installation Art in Close-Up
Minimal Art and Artists In the 1960s and After
Colourfield Painting
Land Art DVD, TV documentary
Andy Goldsworthy DVD, TV documentary
The Erotic Object: Sexuality in Sculpture From Prehistory to the Present Day
Sex in Art: Pornography and Pleasure in Painting and Sculpture
Postwar Art
Sacred Gardens: The Garden in Myth, Religion and Art
Glorification: Religious Abstraction in Renaissance and 20th Century Art
Early Netherlandish Painting
Leonardo da Vinci
Piero della Francesca
Giovanni Bellini
Fra Angelico: Art and Religion in the Renaissance
Mark Rothko: The Art of Transcendence
Frank Stella: American Abstract Artist
Jasper Johns
Brice Marden
Alison Wilding: The Embrace of Sculpture
Vincent van Gogh: Visionary Landscapes
Eric Gill: Nuptials of God
Constantin Brancusi: Sculpting the Essence of Things
Max Beckmann
Caravaggio
Gustave Moreau
Egon Schiele: Sex and Death In Purple Stockings
Delizioso Fotografico Fervore: Works In Process 1
Sacro Cuore: Works In Process 2
The Light Eternal: J.M.W. Turner
The Madonna Glorified: Karen Arthurs

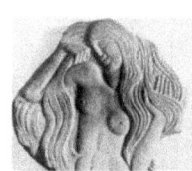
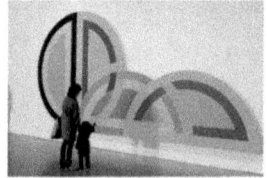
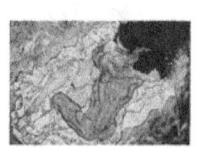
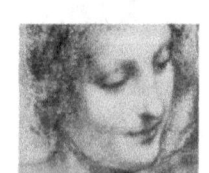
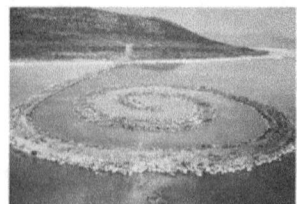

LITERATURE

J.R.R. Tolkien: The Books, The Films, The Whole Cultural Phenomenon
J.R.R. Tolkien: Pocket Guide
Tolkien's Heroic Quest
The *Earthsea* Books of Ursula Le Guin
Beauties, Beasts and Enchantment: Classic French Fairy Tales
German Popular Stories by the Brothers Grimm
Philip Pullman and *His Dark Materials*
Sexing Hardy: Thomas Hardy and Feminism
Thomas Hardy's *Tess of the d'Urbervilles*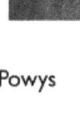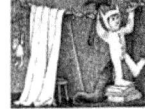
Thomas Hardy's *Jude the Obscure*
Thomas Hardy: The Tragic Novels
Love and Tragedy: Thomas Hardy
The Poetry of Landscape in Hardy
Wessex Revisited: Thomas Hardy and John Cowper Powys
Wolfgang Iser: Essays and Interviews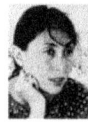
Petrarch, Dante and the Troubadours
Maurice Sendak and the Art of Children's Book Illustration
Andrea Dworkin
Cixous, Irigaray, Kristeva: The *Jouissance* of French Feminism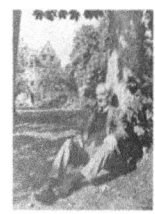
Julia Kristeva: Art, Love, Melancholy, Philosophy, Semiotics and Psychoanalysis
Hélène Cixous I Love You: The *Jouissance* of Writing
Luce Irigaray: Lips, Kissing, and the Politics of Sexual Difference
Peter Redgrove: Here Comes the Flood
Peter Redgrove: Sex-Magic-Poetry-Cornwall
Lawrence Durrell: Between Love and Death, East and West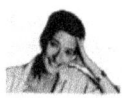
Love, Culture & Poetry: Lawrence Durrell
Cavafy: Anatomy of a Soul
German Romantic Poetry: Goethe, Novalis, Heine, Hölderlin
Feminism and Shakespeare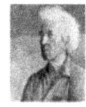
Shakespeare: Love, Poetry & Magic
The Passion of D.H. Lawrence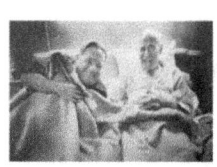
D.H. Lawrence: Symbolic Landscapes
D.H. Lawrence: Infinite Sensual Violence
Rimbaud: Arthur Rimbaud and the Magic of Poetry
The Ecstasies of John Cowper Powys
Sensualism and Mythology: The Wessex Novels of John Cowper Powys
Amorous Life: John Cowper Powys and the Manifestation of Affectivity (H.W. Fawkner)
Postmodern Powys: New Essays on John Cowper Powys (Joe Boulter)
Rethinking Powys: Critical Essays on John Cowper Powys
Paul Bowles & Bernardo Bertolucci
Rainer Maria Rilke
Joseph Conrad: *Heart of Darkness*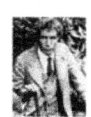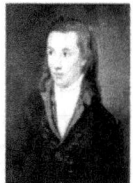
In the Dim Void: Samuel Beckett
Samuel Beckett Goes into the Silence
André Gide: Fiction and Fervour
Jackie Collins and the Blockbuster Novel
Blinded By Her Light: The Love-Poetry of Robert Graves
The Passion of Colours: Travels In Mediterranean Lands
Poetic Forms

POETRY

Ursula Le Guin: Walking In Cornwall
Peter Redgrove: Here Comes The Flood
Peter Redgrove: Sex-Magic-Poetry-Cornwall
Dante: Selections From the Vita Nuova
Petrarch, Dante and the Troubadours
William Shakespeare: Sonnets
William Shakespeare: Complete Poems
Blinded By Her Light: The Love-Poetry of Robert Graves
Emily Dickinson: Selected Poems
Emily Brontë: Poems
Thomas Hardy: Selected Poems
Percy Bysshe Shelley: Poems
John Keats: Selected Poems
Joh n Keats: Poems of 1820
D.H. Lawrence: Selected Poems
Edmund Spenser: Poems
Edmund Spenser: Amoretti
John Donne: Poems
Henry Vaughan: Poems
Sir Thomas Wyatt: Poems
Robert Herrick: Selected Poems
Rilke: Space, Essence and Angels in the Poetry of Rainer Maria Rilke
Rainer Maria Rilke: Selected Poems
Friedrich Hölderlin: Selected Poems
Arseny Tarkovsky: Selected Poems
Arthur Rimbaud: Selected Poems
Arthur Rimbaud: A Season in Hell
Arthur Rimbaud and the Magic of Poetry
Novalis: Hymns To the Night
German Romantic Poetry
Paul Verlaine: Selected Poems
Elizaethan Sonnet Cycles
D.J. Enright: By-Blows
Jeremy Reed: Brigitte's Blue Heart
Jeremy Reed: Claudia Schiffer's Red Shoes
Gorgeous Little Orpheus
Radiance: New Poems
Crescent Moon Book of Nature Poetry
Crescent Moon Book of Love Poetry
Crescent Moon Book of Mystical Poetry
Crescent Moon Book of Elizabethan Love Poetry
Crescent Moon Book of Metaphysical Poetry
Crescent Moon Book of Romantic Poetry
Pagan America: New American Poetry

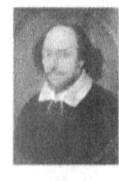
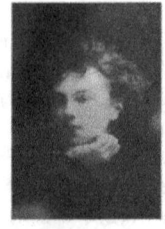
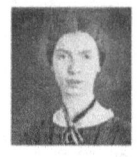
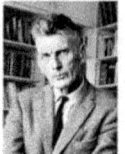
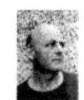
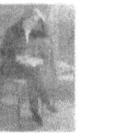
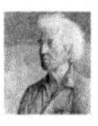
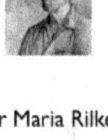
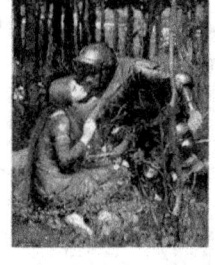
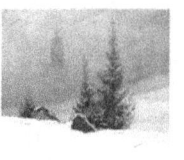
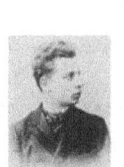
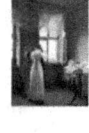
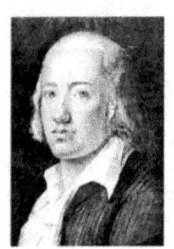
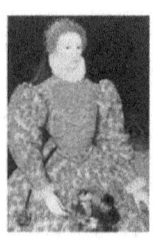

MEDIA, CINEMA, FEMINISM and CULTURAL STUDIES

J.R.R. Tolkien: The Books, The Films, The Whole Cultural Phenomenon
J.R.R. Tolkien: Pocket Guide
The *Lord of the Rings* Movies: Pocket Guide
The Cinema of Hayao Miyazaki
Hayao Miyazaki: *Princess Mononoke*: Pocket Movie Guide
Hayao Miyazaki: *Spirited Away*: Pocket Movie Guide
Tim Burton : Hallowe'en For Hollywood
Ken Russell
Ken Russell: *Tommy*: Pocket Movie Guide
The Ghost Dance: The Origins of Religion
The Peyote Cult

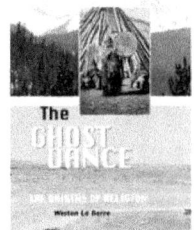
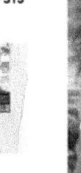

Cixous, Irigaray, Kristeva: The *Jouissance* of French Feminism
Julia Kristeva: Art, Love, Melancholy, Philosophy, Semiotics and Psychoanalysis
Luce Irigaray: Lips, Kissing, and the Politics of Sexual Difference
Hélene Cixous I Love You: The *Jouissance* of Writing
Andrea Dworkin
'Cosmo Woman': The World of Women's Magazines
Women in Pop Music
HomeGround: The Kate Bush Anthology
Discovering the Goddess (Geoffrey Ashe)
The Poetry of Cinema
The Sacred Cinema of Andrei Tarkovsky
Andrei Tarkovsky: Pocket Guide
Andrei Tarkovsky: *Mirror*: Pocket Movie Guide
Andrei Tarkovsky: *The Sacrifice*: Pocket Movie Guide
Walerian Borowczyk: Cinema of Erotic Dreams
Jean-Luc Godard: The Passion of Cinema
Jean-Luc Godard: *Hail Mary*: Pocket Movie Guide
Jean-Luc Godard: *Contempt*: Pocket Movie Guide
Jean-Luc Godard: *Pierrot le Fou*: Pocket Movie Guide
John Hughes and Eighties Cinema
Ferris Bueller's Day Off: Pocket Movie Guide
Jean-Luc Godard: Pocket Guide
The Cinema of Richard Linklater
Liv Tyler: Star In Ascendance
Blade Runner and the Films of Philip K. Dick
Paul Bowles and Bernardo Bertolucci
Media Hell: Radio, TV and the Press
An Open Letter to the BBC
Detonation Britain: Nuclear War in the UK
Feminism and Shakespeare
Wild Zones: Pornography, Art and Feminism
Sex in Art: Pornography and Pleasure in Painting and Sculpture
Sexing Hardy: Thomas Hardy and Feminism

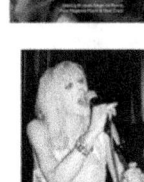
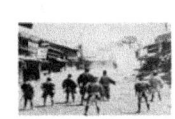
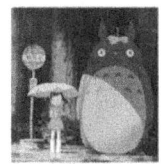
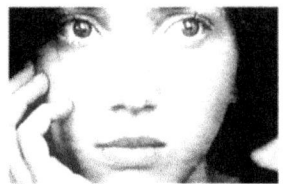

The Light Eternal is a model monograph, an exemplary job. The subject matter of the book is beautifully organised and dead on beam. (Lawrence Durrell)
It is amazing for me to see my work treated with such passion and respect. (Andrea Dworkin)

CRESCENT MOON PUBLISHING
P.O. Box 1312, Maidstone, Kent, ME14 5XU, Great Britain. www.crmoon.com

cresmopub@yahoo.co.uk   www.crescentmoon.org.uk